The Only 21 Stories
You Will Ever Need to Be Successful
in Life & Business

From hardship to a purposeful life
How to be the best version of yourself

Compiled
By
Lucinda Douglas

Publisher: Lucinda Douglas

Cover designer & final editor: Richard van Bruinnessen

Corrector: Allison Ross, Cape Town (SA)

Photo: Ian Schneider

Table of Contents

Foreword

Are these the only 21 stories you will ever need to read in order to succeed in life and business? In a manner of speaking; yes. Even though the individual circumstances and experiences differ, the common thread running through all 21 stories is perseverance, tenacity, triumph and satisfaction through sacrifice and service and more often as a result of deep personal pain. The key is not in denying who we have been but acknowledging that which we are becoming.

A line in one of my favorite songs 'Long Walk' by Jill Scott says: 'Your background it ain't squeaky clean, shit; sometimes we all have to swim upstream." We are all swimming upstream from something, someone, some situation...the muscles we build as we navigate the turbulence empowers and affords a deeper insight. Only personal experience can bring enabling one to illuminate the way for others in diverse ways ...even sometimes just by sheer existing.

Hide not from mistakes nor shy away from imperfections for they do not diminish who we are but if allowed, provides each with a distinct flavor that would only increase one in value.

Rauf Abdul captures it so succinctly, in his analogy of the twenty dollar bill. It didn't lose its value regardless of the wear and tear it had experienced. Everybody still wanted, why? It could still do what a twenty dollar is supposed to do regardless. And think, in the right hand under the right care and supervision, 20 can become 40, 40 60... 60 80... and so on and so on and so on...

Ireti Doyle, Nigerian award winning actress

The Only 21 Stories

This Truth of Mine
Terré Holmes

When I was seventeen, my mother gave me the gift of her sobriety and it was the best gift she could have ever given me, coupled with the power of the truth. My mother sobering up meant that she was finally admitting that she had a problem and that it was much bigger than her. From this decision, I would learn that we cannot free ourselves from a bondage we are unwilling to accept exists.

The truth used to bring me great sorrow. I would sob lonely, gut wrenching cries where the tears flowed like a river and each next breath seemed almost impossible to take. It was a cry that wouldn't cease and left my head pounding and my heart aching. I now realize that I was wounded and when we are still wounded from the pain of our past, it's difficult to talk about it and therefore, very implausible to overcome it.

My mother and father became addicts while in their youth. His drug of choice was heroine. Hers; alcohol and crack cocaine and though I carried the guilt and shame of being their daughter for years, none of this was my fault. I had done nothing wrong, but it would take over half of my lifetime to accept this truth.

Both of my parents were born during the 50's on the East Side of Cleveland, Ohio in similar homes to hard working parents. Both becoming habitual drug users before I was ever thought of. So, it was only logical that bringing a child into the world, wouldn't necessarily change that, but I would spend many years wishing that it had.

Their addictions were never about me, but I did not know that at the time. Honestly, there was so much to their stories that I didn't know and therefore, I didn't quite get them. Like an unfinished puzzle, it's hard to see the entire picture when there are pieces missing. My parents' lives were like those pieces to me. I couldn't really understand how or why people would choose to be parents and then abandon their responsibilities. I spent many sleepless nights wondering what could have happened to them to cause them to neglect and abandon me in more ways than physical and why wasn't I enough for them to finally 'get it together'?

My feelings of inadequacy caused me a lot of heartache. No one had to hurt me, because I caused enough damage on my own. In fact, I was my own worst enemy and deemed myself worthless. I didn't just tell myself this, it played out in my life in multiple ways and in my mind for over twenty years.

Abuse

When you believe you are worthless you will do unthinkable things to yourself and anything that causes you pain and prevents you from looking at yourself in the mirror the next day, falls into that category. As a result of my parents' addictions, I internalized the pain and allowed it to overcome me. Everyone deals with pain differently. When you deny that it exists, you cover it up with drugs and alcohol, gambling or food addictions and even sex. Both sex and overspending became my pain killers and like an addict, true to form, the more I indulged, the more I wanted.

I was twelve years old when I had my first sexual encounter. It was with a young man who lived in our apartment complex. Little did I know, but my mother had started experimenting with drugs about a year prior to that. So it gave me plenty of time to do some experimenting of my own. She was never home and when she was, she slept so hard that a tsunami could hit and she would peacefully ride the wave as if nothing had ever happened. Her new addiction served as the catalyst for what would become my new addiction.

At first, I was having sex simply because I was curious and thought I loved him. Imagine that, a twelve year old in love. I just knew that if I gave him my body that he would give me the love I craved for in return, but I was wrong and not only was I wrong with him, I would spend the next twenty or more years of my life being wrong about who I was, my value, and what I had to give up in order to be on the receiving end of love.

Have you ever heard that hurt people, hurt people? I learned that not only do they hurt people they hurt themselves the most. I know this because I abused myself in more ways than you know. I destroyed relationships, my finances, and abused my body. I judged myself harshly and measured my success by the success of others. Not knowing then that there is no comparison between the sun and the moon. They both shine when they are supposed to.

Retrospect, forgiveness and understanding

There came a time in my life when I realized that in order for me to heal the hurt of my past I had to begin to let go of the pain that had brought me to some of the darkest moments of my life. Like my mother, I had to admit that I was powerless and asked God to intervene on my behalf and replace my destructive thoughts and dangerous behavior, first with love for myself and next with forgiveness.

I had began the journey of forgiving my parents years prior. I was helping others to transform their lives through my work on forgiveness, when one day it hit me. The person I needed to forgive the most was staring back at me in the mirror. I wept like a baby from this revelation and cradled myself with loving arms. The healing was finally beginning.

Overtime, I learned not to greet myself with judgement, but with understanding. Life had been tough for me. I had endured a lot and I had been forced to learn a lot on my own. I wasn't making excuses, I was merely stating my truth, but it was a truth that I wanted to put behind me. I wanted to tell a different story. A story of overcoming. A story of hope. A story of redemption.

Yes, I had been bruised along the way, but I wasn't broken. I could choose to wallow in the past or create a brighter future and allow my pain to fuel my purpose, find the message in my mess and the blessings amidst the bruising.

The blessings were there and through my struggles, I also learned that my story is a gift, not for me, but to be given away to others. So I choose today to put pen to paper and hold microphones to my lips whenever I am asked, so that I can offer someone else the hope I didn't always have, but that I certainly have now. Thank God for forgiveness. Thank God for second chances.

About the Author

Terré Holmes (United States) is a serial-preneur, master business strategist, world traveler, mentor to women globally, an expert on resiliency, as well as a human development coach and enthusiast. She lives just outside of Washington, DC and when she's not traveling, writing, teaching, speaking, or running one of her businesses, you can find her in the kitchen whipping up something tasty and adventurous.

Fortune Favours The Brave
Rauf Abdul

I am a husband, a father, a son, and a brother. I am an uncle, a nephew, a cousin, and a friend. I am a researcher, teacher, speaker, and synergistic HRM consultant. I'm an experienced instructor. I hold a Doctorate in Philosophy degree in the field of HRM. I am not a great cricketer; I am a klutz. I am one who loves to help others, and I believe in one God. I am a sports freak and a smart phone junkie. I am blessed with amazing family and friends. I am strong, but an allergy sufferer. I am one who loves to laugh. I am happy. And I am not, what a lot of people would think, lucky to be born into a privileged class. I made it thus far because I told myself one thing: I am not a loser; no matter what, I can conquer whatever I wish. I am.

But I didn't decide to become a teacher and researcher. Amazingly, it just happened. I believe success is a product of great dreams, determination to do something, and the great resolve to achieve it.

Christopher Reeve said: 'So many of our dreams at first seem impossible, then they seem improbable, and then, when we summon the will, they soon become inevitable.'

Lupita Nyong'O puts it this way: 'No matter where you're from, your dreams are valid.'

My story starts with my first-ever formal conversation with my dad during a spring afternoon over an English cup of tea. I have many stories, but this is one that defines my life journey and one that I will carry with me until my last day.

My father was a school teacher in Burewala, a small town in Pakistan and his one single dream was to provide his children with the best education possible. Like many others, I was determined to carve out a better life for myself. My dad, a strict and authoritarian man, asked me what I would like to do now that I had completed secondary school (remember, I was sixteen). It was a pleasant surprise for me as he hardly gave us any choices. I lived in a culture with hardly any freedom, few choices, and limited exposure to the world outside of school. I took a deep breath and replied that I would love to start a business.

He reacted in his (typically) over-protective style that he did not ask about my work interests, but about my study interests. More specifically, he wanted to know whether I would prefer to pursue an engineering degree or a medical science degree. I said no to both.

I was young with hardly any exposure to the complex practical world, but I was very sure that engineering or medicine was not part of my career aspirations. It wasn't easy, but I convinced my dad that if I wasn't allowed to start a business, business administration was the only field I would study. I am grateful for parents who lovingly allowed me to pursue my dreams, even when it wasn't what they had in mind for me. I completed a PhD in HRM at a world-renowned Dutch university. I then reached a leadership position at one of the top international Business Schools in the Netherlands at a young age.

Step by step

It is true that fortune favours the brave, but it is never just sheer luck. You must not only dream big, but also build your dreams, step by step, with determination and hard work. It comes down to making the right choices at the right times. I remember wanting a marketing job at a big multinational company after my MBA. Instead, I ended up teaching BBA students in a commerce college. In an economy with the highest level of unemployment, even today I am willing to take an entry-level job despite holding the highest academic degree and best possible career position at this moment. This attitude was the very reason I accepted my first-ever less attractive academic position, which completely transformed my thought philosophy. I remember there were several of my BBA students older than me, including a married man and father of one-year old son.

I did my best during my first few years of teaching and did not compromise the quality of my work, but I soon realised I needed to sharpen my research and teaching skills if I wanted to reach academic heights. I decided to obtain a research degree from a foreign university. Excited that my little savings could afford me a plane ticket and cover my expenses for the first few months, I was accepted at one of the renowned UK universities. But the sheer disappointment struck when my visa was rejected for no obvious reasons.

Distraught, my determination to pursue a research degree from a reputable western university remained resolute. I believe in positive thinking as suggested by this great quote: 'I am capable, I am strong. If I believe in myself, I can turn my dreams into a plan, and my plan into my reality.' Within one year, I managed to get a 100% scholarship for a four-year research degree from a university with a great track record for research and higher education in beautiful Holland.

Milestones versus destination

I remember calling one of my favourite MBA teachers for advice before leaving for Holland. To his dismay, I outrightly rejected the only piece of advice he offered: 'Rauf, please do not resign from your current job.' He thought that completing further education or finding a new job might not prove easy, especially in a different culture far away from home. But I knew what I was up for and I said, 'Sorry, sir, I can't accept this piece of advice as I am ready to burn the bridges and not look back.' I was clear that if I couldn't manage to find a similar job, then I did not deserve to have this job. This decision helped me set a principle of moving forward and never looking back. It may seem difficult at times, but eventually you will reach your destination. There is no shortcut to real success and if most things in life is a piece of cake, either there is something wrong with the direction or the destination. A clear direction not only helped me to achieve some important milestones in my life, but also the great success I am enjoying now.

It is important to mention that people define success in different ways. For some, it is having a big bungalow, an SUV, or becoming a billionaire. This is neither achievement nor success in my dictionary. There is difference between milestones and destination. Some people run after achieving simple milestones and never figure out real destinations in life. I would like to share an example of the life objective of a nine-year-old David Warren who invented the black box. His father died in the first-ever air plane crash in Australia. He made every effort to find out what happened, but there was no device to record that flight for clues to what might have gone wrong. He decided to create this device, studied engineering, and in 1956, invented the black box. This device was first used in 1962 in an Australian flight and proceeded to solve airplane crashes and improve airline safety around the world. Mr Warren lived and died achieving this great life objective and will be remembered forever for his invention. While he might have owned a big house and great car, this was not the destination for his life journey. Remember, according to Anthony Robbins: 'It's not about the goal. It's about growing to become the person that can accomplish that goal.'

True value

What I learned in my short career is that there is no difference in each human being's ability to achieve something. Anyone can achieve anything, but it all depends on the efforts, commitment, and hard work. This is an amazing opportunity to share a story from an unknown source about true value. A public speaker started off his lecture by holding up a $20 bill. In the room of 200 participants, he asked: 'Who would like this $20 bill?' Hands started going up. He said: 'I am going to give this $20 to one of you but first, let me do this.' He proceeded to crumple the dollar bill up. He then asked: 'Who still wants it?' Still the hands were up in the air. 'Well', he replied, 'What if I do this?' And he dropped it on the ground and started to grind it into the floor with his shoe. He picked it up, now all crumpled and dirty. 'Now who still wants it?' Still the hands went into the air. 'My friends, you have all learned a very valuable lesson. No matter what I did to the money, you still wanted it because it did not decrease in value. It was still worth $20. Many times in our lives, we are dropped, crumpled, and ground into the dirt by the decisions we make and the circumstances that come our way. We feel as though we are worthless. But no matter what has happened or what will happen, you will never lose your real value.'

The story teaches us that everyone is special. Like me, many people think that their stories are not worth sharing but remember that if you remain true to who you are and don't copy someone else, your story will be a special story worthy to be shared. Be a genuine you. 'All our dreams can come true, if we have the courage to pursue them', said Walt Disney.

As a one final thought, it's interesting to note that we never learn from our successes, we always learn from our failures. Our learning will stop if we only have successes in life. Watch a kid trying to walk. Every time he falls, he learns something and tries again. When he finally takes his first solid steps without falling, you can see his face filled with joy at the victory. I fail to understand why people look for overnight success. You will not be able to find even a single success story without any difficulties and setbacks in life. Those who persevere receive rewards without measure. 'The greatest danger for most of us is not that our aim is too high and we miss it, but that it is too low and we reach it', according to Michelangelo.

About the Author

Rauf Abdul (Pakistan) is a teacher, researcher, education philanthropist and consultant. He holds a PhD in Human Resource Management (HRM) in addition to an MBA and MSc in Business. His main focus in research is on issues related to HRM. He is married and has a two-year-old son.

Booze Interrupted
Peggy-Sue Figueira

She was dead now, and I had not been able to save her. From the day I first saw her at a friend's birthday party in February of 2002, I was smitten. Her name was Tami and she was simply beautiful. She was tall, with a handsome face, chiseled jaw line, scruffy shoulder length hair, brown with blond streaks, and an attitude blend of arrogant shyness.

I had arrived rather intoxicated, but that was nothing exceptional for me. I was in top form and was in the mood for a party. I drank a lot most days, mainly in the evening, as I had a job. Weekends I first went to work-out at the gym and as soon as the Saturday chores were done, I would start drinking. Of course, there were comments about the frequency of my drinking, sometimes jokingly and sometimes more seriously. My answer was a steadfast, 'I work hard, I play hard'. Truthfully, I had started worrying about my increasing use of alcohol too.

I started drinking when I was 18 years old which was quite late in comparison to other kids my age. I had been too afraid before, since people who drank alcohol according to my father were debauched. Sinners. Besides, there was no opportunity to go out and drink. I was never allowed to go anywhere. Strict rules applied at home, and he ruled with an iron rod.

How it started

So, one of the very first times I had an opportunity to drink, we had sneakily gone to an underground nightclub in Durban, South Africa, near the beachfront. The club was called Zodiac. It was 1983. The music was pumping, the people dressed so extravagantly, dressing 'freaky' was all the rage. Dyed and teased hair, clothing chains, bare chested, zig-zag luminous make-up. It was just magical, and I was sold immediately. One entrance fee, unlimited booze.

Fast forward a number of years. It was 1989, I was living in Yeoville, a suburb of Johannesburg and by now I was drinking so much, that even my drinking, diet pill popping and weed smoking, LSD taking friends were concerned. I was extremely depressed on and off, and only my drinking career had really taken off. I worked as a personnel consultant in downtown Johannesburg, and I can't even count the number of times I had to sleep on the toilet floor during working hours, or that I took a taxi home to nap, to be able to rush back to work. Clearly this was career sabotage.

I had already undergone one suicide attempt, because my then girlfriend Ali had decided to leave me as a result of my behavior around drinking, my rather spending time with drinking buddies than at home with her. I would come home wasted, convinced it was none of her business. I was outraged that she chose to leave me, and extremely miserable. I had no idea what to do to fix the immense feeling of emptiness that I suffered. I ended up at the ER at the hospital where my stomach was pumped from an overdose of pills that I had found in her medicine cabinet. I got into all sorts of scrapes - like arriving unannounced and uninvited at my ex's house, falling into bed there, and getting a beating from the new girlfriend when she arrived home after a night shift. I was fifteen kilograms overweight from booze, I had a permanent hangover, I was a mess.

Someone suggested to me to try Alcoholics Anonymous. I did, I went to a few meetings but I had no clue how it worked. Around that time, I had also accepted the responsibility of looking out for my younger sister, who moved in with us, so on all fronts it was really time to stop the booze. And I did. But with no treatment and no working on my underlying issues. However, I stayed sober, and truthfully my life did improve, even though I was on what I now call 'marijuana maintenance', and I dropped the occasional cap of acid (LSD). My career took off, and I climbed the corporate ladder in the marketing of magazines. I started studying Marketing Management, and my weight normalized.

Is this all there is?

Around 1993, my partner of four years Lee, my young sister and I agreed to move to The Netherlands. There was too much political unrest in South Africa. The chance of good education for my sister in Europe and my desire to fall pregnant were on the long list of motivating factors for this move. Once the decision was taken we left the country within three months. What a shock to arrive in cold, wet, miserable, rainy Holland. Nevertheless, I was grimly determined, we had to make this work.

Life was good or, so it looked and we even had bought a house. I had been trying to fall pregnant with medical intervention (insemination), and it just wasn't happening. Nineteen months later I was beside myself with grief when I got my periods yet again. I decided to stop this process. I could feel that Lee was less interested in the pregnancy and that there was an emotional gap growing between us. Then, my girlfriend of ten years, Lee, announced that she was moving back to South Africa. Without me.

This was honestly the beginning of the end for me. I know now that I was not able to recover from this betrayal, this feeling of not belonging anywhere, and again I was outraged, and resentful beyond words. Fueled by anger and grief I went on a workaholism bender. Day and night, I was at the office, I sometimes even slept on the couch at the office. I travelled a lot for work, mainly to the USA. I was depressed and angry and extremely vulnerable and I had no way of figuring what to do to change the feelings of sadness and hopelessness that I had inside.

Woman of my dreams

Then my encounter in 2002 happened, I met the woman of my dreams. Tami, my soulmate. She touched my heart like I had never experienced before. Finally, I had found someone as intense as I was, I felt like I had known her forever, she needed me, and I felt complete. Our life was a roller-coaster of dinners, sports, eating healthily and feeling ridiculously in love. Until she started cheating on me, and left me, from one day to the next. Over the next five years, even after our rather spectacular wedding this happened at least three times.

I fell into an abyss of depression and my drinking escalated. My wife hated the drinking but could use it to justify her behavior. On each occasion that we reconciled, we would do crazy stuff like fly to South Africa on a whim, and summer vacation there. On one of these trips in 2005, hanging out with friends of friends, an upside-down plate was passed around, with on it lines of cocaine and 'cat' (methcathinone, the poor man's cocaine). I was honestly shocked that Tami wanted to try some, since she had always insisted she was anti-drugs and hated the fact that I drank too much.

From that day forth everything in our lives changed. She morphed into an insatiable drug imbiber. I recall feeling a deep sense of despair, even though I was using too, I saw that this really tapped into a core need she had. I felt then that I had really lost her. In fact, that first weekend it looked like we lost her to death, she had used so much that at some stage she turned blue in the face and lips, and she was 'lights out'. Some long-time users that were at the drug den where we were, thankfully managed to resuscitate her.

Months passed by and our using had reached dangerous proportions. I had used up all of the profit on the house that I had sold. I was not able to work, and we were not able to stop using. We would use five days in a row and try to recover over two days. When we went to sleep at night, our face would ache, and we could hardly sleep from the pain.

After searching aimlessly and without good result online for self-help books to figure out how to stop using, and after months of discussing this with my wife, I went against her wishes and told my sister about the drug use. Within 24 hours I was at an assessment for a drug rehabilitation center in Amsterdam, who based their treatment on the so-called Minnesota Model. Within 72 hours I was in treatment.

It would not be true to say that it was all easy from there on, as I still had a few more rock bottoms left in me. A relapse on alcohol six months after treatment, a two-year relapse cross-addiction to 120 mg valium daily, and the devastating loss of my wife due to divorce. She refused to get help in order to stop using, so I gave her an ultimatum and she did what she knew best to do, find someone else. This time she found herself an admissions manager of a medical practice who had empty prescription pads lying around. Sadly, this stage of her life catapulted her into the last and final eight years of her tragic using life. She died aged 38.

It has taken me twelve years to find myself. Tami was dead now and I had not been able to save her, God knows I tried.

I can change

What I learned is that I had the disease of addiction, that it was not relevant what I used, that it would manifest in all areas of my life, different substances, but also behaviors. That the disease of addiction was progressive and chronic. That I needed a spiritual solution and complete abstinence from all mood and mind-altering drugs. And I still felt as if I had been amputated being without Tami. I even negotiated with God- I would have been happy if I could have had her as my child, as long as I could have her in my life.

The biggest gift I have received from my experience with addiction is the conviction that I could change. As do others. To help destigmatize addiction. That what happened to me can and does happen to anyone. Now I am able to help addicts and their family members to turn their lives around.

Today I am a successful entrepreneur, in the field of addiction services. I have done two seasons of a national Dutch Television show on addiction called 'Addicted', where I did TV drug & alcohol Interventions. A year later I was the therapist in the TV show 'Utopia'. I have become a household name in the field of addiction and recovery in The Netherlands.

And the woman of my dreams, she has become the woman in my dreams. She is in a better place now.

About the Author

Peggy-Sue Figueira is a South African-Dutch motivational speaker, addiction counselor and international drug interventionist. She is the founder of a successful business offering addiction services and works closely with clinics all over the world. She lives in Amsterdam.

Oops, I Did It Again
Mirella Eickhof

Oops, I did it again. He fell down, dead, and I immediately shut down my emotions. Such a totally automatic reaction. Guess this was still in my system.

That was six years ago when my partner in crime and life was running at one of the treadmills at our local gym. I was - fanatically, as always - exercising in front of him at the cross trainer when suddenly and unintentionally (or was it?) I looked behind and watched him fall to the floor. To me it felt like it happened in slow motion. In reality, it was quick and with a huge smack. 'This is serious!' someone screamed. In a split second while his life was being drawn out of his body, I decided to lock up my emotions and myself. He's dead. Time to move on.

It surprised me that I could switch attitudes so easily. Yeah, I have always been a survivor. After incest, abandoned by my parents, educating myself since the age of fourteen, moving to six different high schools, I learned to be a tough cookie. I was hard (mostly on myself), strict, and independent. I could always rely on myself. Didn't need anybody. No one could come close. Body and mind separated.

As a teenager, my life was divided. On the one side, insecure and feeling like a stranger at all the schools that I hardly attended. And there was Mirella Two who was the queen of the nightlife. Dancing, always out, walking alone in the city streets at night. Hanging with people much, much older, fellow students envied me. They only saw the 'pleasure' life. The downside was that nobody at home, if there even was a home, could care less where I was.

I didn't feel sorry for myself. I just grew up quickly. I was and still am a believer that all things in life happen for a reason. Call it 'lessons to be learned'. Luckily in those wild days, I always knew exactly what I wanted and what I didn't want. I lived by my own rules. I didn't drink, or smoke. I had high standards and clear values. That was my lifesaver. But I also manipulated people. Yes, that made me strong, harsh, and almost untouchable. But inside I was vulnerable. Most people didn't notice. My challenging childhood made me do things differently. Like hitchhiking, even when I had to walk just three streets further. As I grew older, I chose a different direction. Writing my story, I wonder…Did I choose to do this? Or did life and its opportunities just happen again?

I got pregnant unexpectedly at 22. After eight months of unwillingness to accept this little one inside of me, my baby girl was born. What a surprise! I remember my first two sentences. 'Is this a baby?' And 'She is mine.' I turned 180 degrees. Before the birth, I plotted my own plan. Back to college, working towards my career while the father should raise this child. My pregnancy was kept a secret and neither the baby's father nor my mum was allowed to tell anyone.

I was good at hiding my belly and I hardly gained any weight, so I carried on working at a disco until seven months pregnant. And once the baby was born, even the people in the street thought we adopted a child since they never saw me pregnant. At that time, some females said I was a child with a child. I still think it's an odd expression.

This baby girl changed my life. She softened me up. The first step to a sweeter Mirella took place.

Steps

Time went by. My life's 'blessings' prepared me for my early years as a career counsellor. It gave me plenty of ammunition to understand other people and the problems they face. As a young girl, I was often surrounded by people, mostly older, who shared their problems, doubts, and death wishes. I am a good listener. This talent is useful in my line of business. And since my own life path wasn't common, not many stories felt shocking or awkward. I understood the person in front of me and didn't judge.

I also knew that for my own personal and professional development, I had to grow further and dig even deeper. This was my second step. I asked my colleague to coach me; to turn me upside down; to break me in order to build me up. Sure, this was heavy and confrontational, but so powerful! Today I am in the position to help others in a similar way.

The third step towards gaining more compassion and kindness happened gradually through the years. When you assess other people, whether for selection or development purposes, you have the responsibility to judge them in a proper way. To treat them respectfully, without prejudice. To offer them insights but also honesty. If there is no person-job-culture fit, there is no fit. Working with people and discovering their talents, values and what motivates them is a rewarding job. They learn from you and, in return, you learn from them.

When I met my lover, the one who died at the gym, another phase in my emotional life occurred. Thanks to him, I learned to be more optimistic. It took many, many years and lots of hard work to look on the bright side. I always manage to get results. Not because of my positive mind-set, which I lacked at first, but because I can work like crazy. I am ambitious and quality driven. Giving up will never be in my vocabulary. Referring to my never-ending efforts to build my own businesses, my daughter used to say: 'Mam, are you your work or is your work you?' I admit. I was a workaholic in those days. Now, I just love my work.

I overcome

In the process of shaping and sharpening my own mind-set, skill, behaviour, and personality, I naturally grew older and became a gentler person. I am still proud of my strong will, independence, determination, and persistence, but I also embrace my patience and friendliness. In my early days, I was allergic to the word 'lovely'. It felt like it described someone who was fragile and easily taken advantage of.

I found it difficult to trust other people. That kept me from opening up. Now I share my stories; my successes and my failures. And do I have plenty of both of them! Why not tell someone about what went wrong? For instance, one of our companies went bankrupt. Against my will, the bank manager persuaded me to personally fund the business because I already owned another successful one. Never, ever put yourself in that position! I paid a high price in money, frustrations, and lessons learnt. I share this bad experience to prevent other entrepreneurs from making the same mistake.

Life still challenges me. The difference nowadays is that I overcome. 'I overcome' is far more positive than 'I survive'. No need to fight, to provoke and to make sure I am the strongest. And if someone takes advantage of my kindness or tries to misuse my openness, then let them be. I am glad to be me.

What doesn't kill you makes you stronger, and that is precisely what happened. You see, my partner didn't die that day in the gym. Like a well organised script, people around him reacted as if on cue. The lady behind the desk who first cried out in fear at the seriousness of the situation, stepped in to resuscitate him. The fellow next to him on the treadmill joined her in the rescue using the Automatic External Defibrillator (AED) to save his life. Great teamwork at the gym kept him alive until the paramedics arrived and took him to hospital. Five bypasses later, he survived.

We were lucky that it happened at that particular place, with an AED and people playing their parts like in a movie. In the middle of all this madness, I remained calm. I motivated the others, who were more in panic, to save his life. Yet, seconds before, I said goodbye to him. My harshness, after all these years of transformation, took me by surprise. Must have been my former coping mechanism kicking in.

You choose

After his recovery, we made new choices. Work was no longer the top priority and we decided how and with whom we liked to spend time. Family and friends became more significant. Since then, we plan something special every month. Boy, does quality time feel good, be it a long weekend or a whole week! Because we're both in favour of learning and self-development, we've attended many workshops and seminars in the Netherlands and abroad. Some training courses took me out of my comfort zone. It was liberating and brought me new insights, which I can use in my work and pass along to others.

When you are an entrepreneur, it is important that you develop certain qualities, like being action oriented, confident, committed, positive, persuasive and knowledgeable. You should have great communication skills and, of course, be determined. Other entrepreneurial abilities that are extremely useful are adaptability and leadership. I advise you to investigate which of these qualities come naturally to you and which you're interested in developing further. Maybe consider partnerships with people who complement your strengths and help you overcome your weaknesses.

And even if you don't own a business, adjusting to change (adaptability) and leadership are necessary life skills. The best thing you can do for yourself is to act. If you're not acting, you're reacting. This is a passive way of living and/or working. You will be better off in the front seat because then no one decides for you. This means you take the lead. You set the goals. You plan. You choose. Whatever happens in life, you are in charge of your emotions and decisions. It is your responsibility to lead the way to your own happiness, career and life.

About the Author

Mirella Eickhof (Netherlands) has been an entrepreneur since 2000. She founded several businesses and learned the hard way to deal with life and business issues. She pursued her dream of having a small organisation, delivering big outcomes with an inner core and a diversified outer circle of consultants. She wrote two books: 'Meten of zweten' and 'Wake up!'. Identifying, encouraging and developing talent is what makes her heart tick. She believes that the right people with the right skills aligned with their motivation and the right values, are empowered, and achieve much more. She is also train-the-trainer of the Wave®, an online assessment tool. She's working successfully as mental and career coach and as a talent & development manager for several international organisations.

Can I Trust?
Remco de Geus

Today I broke down in the forest. Exhausted. Suddenly losing all grip on myself. Surrounded by silent trees and the fading echoes of a distant gunshot. The word suicide crossed my mind. But not today. Today I won't be giving in.

It's just… Sometimes we break down. On our knees, bare and blank as a baby. Moments of surrender. But as any newly born, we have to fight. Fight back. Build moments of resilience and regain that inner force that will pull us through. Giving in is no option. Today there will be no trigger.

Lightning conductor

Childhood echoes paved the way. Growing up in an ordinary Dutch town, I was considered to be causing trouble; behavior that nowadays would be labelled ADHD, CD, or ADD. My mom and I were like oil and fire; whenever she spoke to me or corrected me, there was an explosion waiting to happen. My father was never around, working hard and even the few times when he was at home, he was busy fixing things. I had a brother who was the exact opposite of me; a bright kid at school, independent and disciplined. Growing up with him felt like a boxing match that I lost time and time again. You probably guessed it by now: I felt as if nobody understood me. Perhaps they couldn't give me what I needed, or maybe it was because I hadn't yet been taught properly how to deal with emotions. Either way, the continued urge to be noticed combined with a severe lack of love and connection created an internal explosive mixture.

Fitness became my lightning conductor and discharge when during adolescence, I went searching for that which I felt was missing. Slowly I became addicted to working out. The bullied and belittled schoolyard boy was growing into a body builder and a martial arts practitioner at a professional level. I became a respected fitness manager and personal trainer and, because of my strength, I took side jobs as a bouncer and personal body guard.

The crash

The echoes of the previous years slightly slipped away and my existence took shape. I started to study and a beautiful woman walked into my life. I felt I could carry the world on my shoulders. Until that Monday morning in June 2015. The day that would change my life forever. As in a film, I can precisely evoke the scenes as if witnessing someone else. I was in my car on my way to have lunch with a friend and took a left turn coming off the highway, when suddenly I saw a car coming straight at me. I still see the driver's widened eyes and his terrified look. Then a deafening crash immediately followed by complete silence. Not a single echo to be heard.

After five days in the Intensive Care Unit, I regained consciousness and fully began to realize what had happened. I was in a terrible accident. They had to push back my stomach and other organs in their proper positions. I could not sleep. An indescribable pain fell over me like a suffocating blanket. My heart began pounding and sweat was running everywhere. I realized that I - my whole system - was fighting for life. My life. I constantly called the nurse for more medication. I thought that my body was abandoning me. I begged, I promised to God, to myself, and to anybody who would listen that 'If I survive this night then I will… because I want…'

The accident has been the best and the worst thing that has ever happened to me. My body was literally shaken beyond repair and, consequently, I lost my work, my hobbies, my recognition, my coping mechanisms… essentially, my life. I even had to learn how to walk again. This process forced me to focus on myself as a person rather than to focus only on my body. I learned that I have a willpower that can help me through the darkest periods in my life. And that I can utilize the skills of my previous life in many different ways.

Three years after the crash, its echoes are still very much alive. I am still in the process of medical rehabilitation, but I have picked up the pieces of my life. I am working as a teacher with students who have to deal with troubling experiences themselves. I was also able to continue my work as a personal trainer, and I realize that personal development never stops. And when you keep growing, you can give much more to others.

Discipline

I learned that the best way to start doing things is to develop habits and rituals that facilitate and to be strict. I had to, for in the first year of my medical rehabilitation, I lost my girlfriend and my job… resulting in a lengthy legal battle with my employer. I had hit rock bottom. My body had let me down and my willpower was going the same direction. Thoughts of putting an end to my life were reoccurring. I had to find a new ritual, a new discipline, a reason to live for. I found the answer. I bought a puppy. The puppy pulled me through; his schedule became my schedule; his training became my training. And I recovered. The puppy became my own personal butterfly effect.

'You have to find meaning in the suffering', says Dr. Viktor Frankl, psychiatrist and holocaust survivor. I agree. I am convinced that in every pain there is something to gain. Look at suffering and learning as conditions to develop as a human being.

For many years, I thought that my ego and identity were based on the number of trophies I won and the control I exercised over my emotions. Until the crash that erased my identity in a second. In that moment when you don't know who you are anymore, the only way out is to find out why you are here. With this in mind, my accident and the path that I followed, I am stronger than ever. Through this I have developed skills so that I can help people grow; people who I otherwise would never have been able to reach or understand.

Trust

In the first year of my rehabilitation, the labor conflict unfolded with my former employer, one that eventually was fought out in court and when even that didn't help, we ended up together at the police station. A good friend told me at that time: 'Forgiving is not about the other, it is about you. Let it go. It takes too much of your energy, and you need that energy for your recovery.'

Forgiving and trusting. Two values I never considered before. I think many of us let anger, fear and hatred prevail. At least I did. Can I forgive? Can I forgive everyone who has hurt me, deceived me, stolen from me, threatened me in any way? The ones who backstabbed me, bullied me, or abandoned me in any way? Turning the echoes of the past down I must admit, it takes time and effort. Trust is not my strongest quality and, looking back, it may have suffered some serious knocks over the years. But I have learned by now that it gives you a lot more energy and space for new things when you let it go, no matter what it is. Stop trying to control everything which actually can't be controlled. Let it go. It is my discovery. It is my treasure which gives me the energy to go on when I need it most. The question that haunts me: could even I be an anchor in someone else's life? Could somebody trust me and could I trust this person completely?

That same friend told me: 'Try to trust in a higher power than yourself. There is a greater plan that you are a part of. First try trusting God. I am convinced that this will bring you peace.' He introduced me to God, the one I was calling out to when I felt I was dying. The acquaintance provides me with a calmness. And there is also the feeling of that warm bath I get when I surround myself with the people that unquestionably call God Father. A feeling that was unknown to me. Therefore, I am willing to try to trust God like they do. And let Him be my guide, my confidant, my inspiration and the Father that can teach me how to forgive and to trust. No more echoes, but a positive trigger and a new start every day. I say yes.

About the Author

Remco de Geus (Netherlands) is a teacher, social worker and personal trainer.

How Did I Get Here?
Laura Peli

When I did my Master's degree, one of my teachers gave us students an assignment: to write a full page about our future life. She said the title was 'How did I get here?' and she wanted us to imagine in details how our life would be ten years later. We had to explain all the steps we undertook to reach our imaginary goal. I thought It was an inspiring task as I had to force myself to picture a successful bright future in a time where everything seemed so far away.

Nearly a decade has passed since that day and here I am. My life turned out to be very different from the one I described on that piece of paper, but I realized how important dreams and goals are when you work on yourself and your career. Now, at 33 years of age, I look back and I ask myself (this time for real) 'How did I get here?'

Growing pains of an ugly duckling

'Laura you are ugly!', my heart stopped beating. How could my mother lie to me saying I was the most beautiful girl in the world, when the other children declared so clearly how unpleasant my face was? I wanted to die. When you are seven years old, and you live in a small town in the middle of Italy knowing nothing about the world, you believe that this is it: you are worthless and you feel hopeless. I grew up watching films from the 80s, and like the majority of kids my age, I wanted to live a life like in a movie, adventurous and challenging. My favorite film was The Goonies: a group of brave kids find an old map and discover a hidden pirate ship and its treasure. My life couldn't be more different: I wasn't even allowed to run until the top of the road without being supervised by an adult. My existence was incredibly frustrating, but I had hidden hopes and dreams to keep me company. I knew that in a way or another I'd find my own pirate treasure.

In order to do so, I had to survive the suburban youngster's life in the best way possible: 'If I cannot be beautiful, I will work on myself to be funny and smart.'

Back in 6th grade, I became my friends' favorite confidant. The fact I was still living in my bud pushed me to improve other sets of skills such as my ability to listen. I found out that people needed attention, they loved to talk about themselves and for the first time in my life, it felt like I was in the right place.

Growing up and getting prettier didn't make things better, when you are a fourteen-year-old girl, the worst thing can happen is to listen to your parents and choose the wrong subjects in high school. If you have never been an Italian teenager you cannot understand how pressured you can feel because of your family. Every choice you make is a family decision: it was like living on an everlasting episode of The Sopranos vs Dawson's Creek. I chose a school focused on Economics and Finance, and I hated it. But I was the top of my class in English, French and Spanish, this is how my love for foreign languages came to light. Eventually, I realized that knowing more languages was the key to open the door between my little town and the rest of the world.

I was in a hurry to explore and learn new things, but my parents had a different opinion: 'When you are eighteen you will do whatever you want with your life. Until then this is our house, these are our rules!' My naivety really made me believe that as soon as I blew my eighteenth candle, they would be happy for me to do whatever I wanted to do. What a gullible little girl I was!

I had to live under my parents' roof for a couple of years more until I completed my Bachelor's degree in Foreign Languages and Arts. The same day I graduated and was crowned with laurel, I booked a one-way flight to London. This is how I believed my life would become an exciting TV series.

E for expat

Being an expat wasn't the same I have imagined. I didn't live in a cool apartment like in the TV show Friends, nor, there was a pub where I would meet my closest friends every day after work. The first flat I lived in was quite dirty, there was no living room and naughty mice would freely run around. I loved it though, because I finally moved abroad and I planted my flag. At that time, I felt it was just a matter of time for my career to take off.

After trying the typical expats' jobs as a waitress, barista, and babysitter I decided it was time to go back to studying.

Since English wasn't my first language I needed more qualifications to win the competition. University life in England was so much better than in Italy. I enjoyed so much preparing presentations, writing essays and reading academic articles. During that period my personal growth reached its peak.

After earning my Master's degree I got a job in events. I still recall the sense of failure and frustration I felt every day after work. I was impressed by the number of mistakes I could make in just eight hours. It was like going back to childhood, feeling useless and lost. The sensation didn't last for long though, as I soon understood that the only way to learn for me, was to make mistakes. That very work experience was the longest learning curve of my career. Painful, but very much needed.

Coaching what art thou?

Let's step back quickly to 2010. When I heard the word coaching for the very first time. I was in a cafe and I met an interesting woman in her fifties, very energetic and positive. She was a professional coach and I thought she was incredibly fascinating. I felt compelled to learn more about coaching because I was sure I had the right qualities to become one sooner or later. For the next few years, I attended several courses, I read tons of books and attended seminars conducted by the most famous coaches of the world. I started practicing coaching while I was working other jobs. I would meet my coachees after work or during lunch breaks, sometimes even on weekends. I juggled between my job and coaching until I opened my company. On July 2016, right after England asked Europe for a divorce, Ni-Cons Consulting Limited was born.

Co-founding Ni-Cons Consulting

'Ni in Chinese means You!' - said Carla while scribbling on her Moleskine – 'In this way, we will offer the best bespoke services, according to the individual strengths and personal profile!' I liked it and it completely resonated with me and my coaching approach: I am passionate about people and I love the fact that each person has different talents and aspirations. Carla and I developed a business to support students and recent graduates to face the world of work but also, through coaching, we have helped anyone who felt stuck in their career path and life.

Carla Ferrero, my business partner, is a clever and witty woman in her early thirties. She lived in China for five years and then moved to the UK to manage the British branch of a Chinese company. Carla has my same drive, aims, and respect, but she's got completely different talents other than a completely different physical appearance. Someone once called us the Yin and the Yang: Carla has an elegant composure and she is incredible in networking, whereas I am much more passionate and I am good in one to one meetings. When we travel across Europe, running Career Workshops in universities and schools, the students enjoy the balance we have. Also, they enjoy the fact that we are just a few years older than they are, in this way the message we send is clear: 'If we made it, you can make it too.'

The ups and downs of a CEO

All that glitters is not (always) gold. Working on your own is great, exciting and it's yours; but the amount of preoccupations and stress is something you have to come to terms with. The lovely sensation of freedom you feel on a Saturday and a Sunday when you work as an employee, it's a pleasure you'll soon forget about. Your business is like your child, and you can never lose the sight of it. Especially at the beginning. I spent the first nine months completely immersed in my new business. Step by step, I have learned to give myself some free time: I made sure I had no access to my emails and phone calls for half a day, twice a week. The first year is the period where I have learned how to cope with my bounds, which is incredibly hard. I have been struggling so much to demonstrate to myself I was strong, that my limits reminded me I was just a human being. As a matter of fact, the following year as a CEO is when I started to forgive myself for not being always insanely up to my expectations.

My journey began with me being an ugly duckling, growing up as the Queen Bee of Mistakes, slowly accepting new challenges such as moving abroad on my own and constantly proving myself.

I can now say that my biggest achievement was to understand that failing is not the opposite of winning.But that failure is part and parcel of success. I still got a long way ahead, and still endless feathers in my cap of flaws. My experience taught me that mistakes are my way to learn and that failure is healthy only if my reaction is: 'That's fine! This is not the right path. Let's try another one.'

About the Author

Laura Peli (Italy) has been living in London for ten years. Born in the green heart of Italy, she is the last of four sisters. Her family is where she learned the essence of Girl Power. She grew up reading books and dreaming a life full of adventures. When she realized her home-town couldn't offer what she wanted, Laura moved to London where food and weather weren't as good as in her home country, but she could finally be challenged as she wished to. With her business partner Carla Ferrero founded Ni-Cons Consulting: they help students to get into the world of work and they also run Women Empowerment workshops, enabling female collaboration in life and business.

Power Play
Lucinda Douglas

Back in 2012, I was on holiday at my sister's place in the South of France, the most beautiful setting you can imagine. I had always found it to be relaxing, spacious and so different from my daily life. One Sunday afternoon, I was fiddling with my smartphone and noticed a number suddenly vanish; the number of the commercial director of a company in Amsterdam whom I had been talking to for a long time. I wanted to add value to this company because I liked the dynamics, so I immediately called the general director and heard myself saying these amazing words: 'I see that your colleague has just vanished off the face of the earth. I want his position. He's done this job for 26 years, day in and day out. I want to straighten things out in one year working for you only three days a week.' Sooner than he could answer, I added that I would be there 48 hours later. So much for my holiday!

The power game

Two days later, I entered a room where seven men welcomed me with raised brows. I introduced myself to the

Board of Directors and explained that I had exactly one hour for this conversation. I made it clear I wanted the post of commercial director because I had gained many years of experience in training, skill building and role playing. After stating what I wanted, I just kept quiet and waited - weak in the knees - for the next move to be made. Now this is where it became interesting. No, I had no experience as a director, but I had told them that I would raise the profits by 40% in one year, and that I could do it by working three days per week while managing a team of 26 people. In the sudden silence that followed, all present were confronted with themselves. I was sharply dressed, looking good and I was talking to them in the same style as men do with one another. As the only woman in the room, I knew I had to step into character, be convincing, and exude confidence, which I did.

While I was jotting down a remark, one of the men cleared his throat, looked my way and said: 'Could you please get us some coffee.' I lifted my eyes and replied with a slight smile: 'No sugar, please.' A new, but now awkward, silence fell. I congratulated myself on handling this power play. My comment had impact. I could very well feel the power game going on in that room. I realised that even though I had some reputation and I was bluffing my way through this meeting, the chances I could pull it off were growing by the second, and so was my confidence. I was tenacious and felt the adrenaline rushing through my veins. I had promised myself that I would not leave this room without this job. After the acclaimed hour, I left with my first director title. This play was won on body language, a challenging spirit and my invisible tenacity. On hearing the story, people would say to me: 'But those were male qualities that you used,' and I would reply: 'So? Under these circumstances I used them to get the job done. I beat them at their own game.' I was a woman in my own right.

Playing along

I was introduced to the European offices of the company, exactly where I wanted to be. I had no office and the meeting room was always cleared when I arrived. I loved the space and having no rules but my own. My teams were predominantly male, and in the beginning, they found it difficult to have me as their boss. They would play with me, trying to reach my female emotions. But I was always firm and to the point because firm and to the point is how I liked to be treated. And by then, the structure was improving and profits were growing. Being a woman was an advantage. How? All my male colleagues thought that I used intuition, knew more, and could see right through them. Somehow, they seemed to think that I possessed the amazing qualities of their wives as well as their own qualities. And I played along.

But not all people were happy; some requested a meeting with the Board of Directors to get rid of me, but my board loved my results so much that my value grew. As I was performing this role for only three days a week, I had two days left to work in my own business. I must admit... it took plenty of time and energy organising the meetings and business plans in different countries, but I got it done. Being firm made all the difference.

During the same year, another company approached me with an amazing proposition. They wanted women board members within their company and asked if I would mentor them. I gladly accepted the challenge and loved working with these women. This project taught me much about myself because I was learning and mentoring at the same time. And the questions they had were my questions, too. I was a glutton, eager to learn, and learning fast.

Cracks

I noticed that I liked the challenge, the power, and the fact that every eye was constantly focused on me. My position gave me status, value and I was having fun. By 06:00 every morning I received the profit results of the previous day. My goodness… it was amazing. But cracks started showing. I discovered something about myself: I am not a person for details. Well, very briefly and then I need to get on with the big idea. And the spreadsheets were getting to me. I even had to learn to read them. This was truly boring and my interest in this part of the business was dwindling.

Around the same time, the owners of the company asked me to redesign the business in the United Kingdom because my approach was working. What an amazing boost for me! The question I asked myself, though, was: 'What was I actually doing right?' I know… no man would say what I am now saying, but I did what came naturally to me so I had never had to question it. I kept order, had fun, played, experimented and gave my honest opinion. In mentoring, one needs to be objective, yet loving and it worked like a bomb. My natural compass took me to limitless heights.

Blessed person

I was running through a few profit and loss sheets one afternoon when one of my managers came to speak with me. He shared with me that he had been a sniper in the armed forces and, once on a global mission, had to eliminate 25 people. He needed to tell someone and I was the one he told. Now, 30 years after the mission, he broke down in tears at my desk. It was not my position that got me into this conversation, nor that fact that I was a woman. It was because of the person I was. I was someone he could trust me with his life and I was taken aback. I didn't say a word when he was telling his story. I just was there, listening and registering. I got him a cup of tea and that was it. Or so I thought. Instead, it turned out to be a deciding moment in my life. I realised in that moment that I would never have to achieve more than what had just taken place at my desk. This, I found, was the highest position anybody could attain. This was the most amazing thing that could ever have happened to me. Just being. Just being was enough.

After this realisation, running a business became easier. I could do it with my eyes closed. I was now traveling between London, Brussels and Amsterdam and I was getting better by the day. But there came a point where I knew I had to let go. This jacket was getting too tight and my time was up. Yes, I could have stayed for years, but I had already accomplished what I had set out to do. You see, after this job I knew that there was not a single thing I could not do. Everything was wide open and my world was huge!

When I left the company after a year, I was one of only three people left on the board. Because my qualities went both ways, I was comfortable with company politics, playing the game at the right level, and making powerful and drastic decisions. This was my playground. Here I could play, transform and develop. When I handed in my company car

- my appreciated Mercedes Benz - I said to my colleague: 'One of the most difficult things in the past year was coping with the power. That was the only part I could not manage. I failed at it.' And I added: 'And so did you.' He had broken down several times, but I saw how men cover each other's backs, never admitting at this level that there was ever anything they could not do.

This one year changed my life and confronted me with my shortcomings. It was fun, but I needed more than only me. Here I turned back to God because I noticed that I was falling short. I reinforced my faith and my belief. And my life now seems to have no limits. I am a very blessed person.

About the Author

Lucinda Douglas (Netherlands) advises, speaks and mentors women worldwide on getting ahead. She has written several books. The day she left the company mentioned in her story, she wrote the management book 'Sales Is Sexy'. Lucinda was born in Cape Town during the South African apartheid era where she learned to transform adversity into success. In 2018, she wrote her autobiography 'Yes You Can Woman', an inspiration for women all over the world. She has several nominations to her name and has been said to be one of the most inspiring women in Europe. She is guest lecturer in entrepreneurship at a private university and well loved by the media.

You Get What You Give
Sylvia Haensel

Can you imagine growing up in one of the most challenging times of Germany? During the fall of the Berlin Wall that separated West from East Germany for more than 28 years? By the time the magical words 'Wir sind das Volk' ('We are the People') had been spoken and the wall fell, I was seventeen years old. And maybe a distant event for some of us living in other continents, for me it was the biggest miracle of my life. This energetic sparkle, thousands of families reunited, an unparalleled happiness and openness was touching a whole nation. Little did I know at that moment that reuniting people and working purposefully together would be the important theme in my life.

I grew up in a county where its people had the reputation of being efficient, always on time, and organized. As a little girl, I had to live up to that. I learnt early that life had many uncertainties in surprise and that I would have to depend on myself and my talents. Over the years, I discovered my gift of easily connecting with people and my determination to take responsibility for my actions. And I felt, I could make a difference.

A while after the reunification, the glimmer vanished. The new Germany was in disarray, trying to balance its two parts in salaries, life standards, pensions, and unemployment. As a 'West Berliner', I started leading a small bank team in former East Germany. I had two local women in my team, who applied for my position but were rejected. Pushed into that management position, I didn't always feel young, wild, and unstoppable; I had countless sleepless nights.

It was the beginning of January in winter. I remember arriving in the dark, way before 8.00 am, parking my old Opel Astra and taking a deep breath for my first day of being a 'not wanted' branch manager. The huge bank building with its impressive big windows made me feel so small. The warm lights inside had already been switched on, but weren't inviting. My knees were shaking, my heart was racing, and my brain was searching for a way or reason to run away. But I didn't. The little war in that bank branch started immediately: East versus West; young versus old; we-always-do-it-like-this versus change. I learnt by using my instinct and through trial and error. And eventually we became a fantastic and successful team, thanks to my personal belief 'You get what you give'.

Discovering my talent

Let's jump forward. Managing a start-up in the Netherlands a decade later, I regularly hired two new interns at a time. I called them my super interns, the lucky chosen ones. Sometimes I only had three applications, but that didn't matter. It was the 'I want only you' message that I wanted to emphasize. My colleagues, responsible for other markets, didn't feel the same way about the interns they hired and ended up complaining about them. My interns were extremely motivated, loyal, worked longer, and together we had lots of fun. I felt happy with my choices. It was only when my HR (Human Resources) colleague in my third management role came up to me after three years and said: 'Well, Sylvia, I don't believe in luck anymore, it's you who always creates this fantastic team around you!' Seeing how other managers hired and fired many employees in short intervals - all so-called lazy or incompetent - I started to believe that I really could have a talent for forming great, successful teams.

Ability meets commitment

In my opinion the best way to measure motivation is by observing how people do their daily tasks. If you notice employees who regularly do what they have been told to do suddenly forget how to do it, how would you react if you were their manager? If what you had in mind was 'Well, I call him or her for a meeting and explain again how to do it right', don't worry, you are not alone. The majority of managers act like that and sometimes it works - short term. But do you really think your employee forgets how to do it right? There are, based on my experience, only two reasons why employees don't do what they're trained for: they can't or they don't want to. It's either lack of competence or lack of engagement. Only if ability meets commitment will the employee do his or her work correctly.

As I mentioned earlier, I was sent to that little bank branch in East Germany. Of the original staff of six women, none of them were happy to be managed by a young woman from Berlin. Demotivation and lack of engagement everywhere and me unsure and paralyzed by the workload. We had four open phone lines. I remember a phone always ringing in the background. Horrible! We had no time during the bank opening hours to attend meetings or even read our mails properly. After three weeks, I knew I had failed to connect us as a team.

Then I had an epiphany. I came up with the idea of team breakfasts on a Friday instead of meetings after a long working day. We would start half an hour earlier than usual, sit around our kitchen table and one by one openly share news or problems in a relaxed atmosphere while we ate. Everybody was listening, criticism was not allowed, only solutions. For my part, I could see what was individually missing: ability or commitment.

By giving people and myself a relaxed place to be heard, to be recognized, and to be taken seriously, we grew together and built a successful team, even with the most 'difficult' colleagues. Soon I was becoming the accepted leader and manager of our team. Instead of getting up with bellyache, I now jumped out of the bed facing the new challenges with a smile, looking forward to seeing them all, my small work-family.

Transparent

Being transparent, not hiding the bitter truth, isn't comfortable at all. It takes a lot of courage to get it out. In my life I learnt very early that I am not perfect. Later I figured it out: nobody is. Accepting that it's ok to be imperfect and being responsible for my actions and my words were some of the best things life has taught me.

One of the management positions I accepted, knowing that the former manager would have to step back into the team.

He was a hard worker, smart, committed and always accurate in performing his task, so I really wanted to keep him. Knowing it would be difficult for both of us, I formed my strategy based on transparency and shared with him extra tasks adapted to his level of knowledge. I also told him that there were no possibilities to climb the carrier ladder for a long time. Being transparent about his future may have been hard at first, but also fair on both sides. Of course, trust takes time and there will be some drawbacks, but within three months we became a great team, respecting each other and facing the challenges of the daily work together.

Still, trust is a long-term project and, like all relationships, needs continuous work.

Trust

I am still thankful for my education and experience as a young professional at my first bank job. We had so many good leaders from which I learnt and to whom I looked up to. Experienced managers who were relaxed and self-confident, who had the right attitude, and didn't need to feed their egos.

One of the managers who shaped me very early was our HR regional director. When he started to take over one hundred branches, he did something very impressive. He took the time to visit all branches and spoke with all employees. Even me, at that time a young bank student. He sat down for twenty minutes and asked questions. 'What is bothering you?' 'What works well?' 'What do you need to do it better?' Can you imagine how important and motivated I felt that a regional director was asking me questions and listening to me? I will never forget how impressed and proud I was when weeks later my little comment was picked up and executed – even if it was just a plant to give more privacy to waiting clients at the cashier.

When I launched the start-up and as well as when I became head of Sales, I used this plan via a kick-off workshop. Using the outcomes of the workshop, I created an open to-do-list of the changes suggested by team members. Before every team meeting, I would refer to open points on the to-do list and give reasons why we were or were not going to implement the changes or I would explain that it would be handled later. This showed the team that every suggestion was recognized and not forgotten, and that their opinions were valued. When your opinion is valued, you are motivated, you are creative, and you start working with commitment for the common target.

This recommendation is not new. All kinds of management books, especially in sales, tell us: listen to your staff! These people have direct customer contact or perform the day-to-day tasks. The guys on the desk, the people who answer customer questions, they are your treasure. My staff gave me important information, showed me what was going right or wrong - and saved me huge consulting fees for external researchers. Knowing this, I've always wondered why CEOs often trust external consultants more than their own staff.

Looking back, I am extremely happy that I accepted my first big challenge of being a branch manager - and that I didn't run away. And you know why not? Along my private and professional path, I met wonderful people who trusted me more than I trusted myself. My self-confidence came only after allowing myself to make plenty of mistakes and learning from them. So, keep on going, don't run away, and trust in your talents. You get what you give!

About the Author

Sylvia Haensel (Germany) is head of Sales at Stellar Data Recovery. She was one of the youngest branch managers at Dresdner Bank, business developer and authorized representative of IKB Deutsche Industriebank AG and managed a Dutch start-up. As a MBA graduate she teaches MBA modules at the CNAM institute in Paris (France) and provides free online finance lessons to students in developing countries e.g. Africa. She speaks and lectures on her experience in business administration and leadership in international study programs. Sylvia lives life with a high degree of authenticity and fun.

From Hero To Zero. And Back Again
Michael Knulst

I have been fortunate to experience some life defining moments. They have helped me to see that the best measure of success is who you are as a person and the value you bring to people's lives.

I was born and raised in a loving family. My father was an entrepreneur and he demonstrated the importance of great work ethics and values as a foundation to success. Despite all his efforts and my mother's support, he still struggled to make a decent living from his business. My father was my role model. Through his business, I learnt the value of working hard, never giving up and being true to my word. I was determined to take on board the lessons that he taught me and to look for help in the areas where he had not been successful.

And there I was, at 33 years of age, a successful sharply dressed businessman in the middle of a room with weird people who were chanting, dancing and hugging. I wondered if I had stepped into the wrong meeting. I was backing out of the room until this hippy lady with beautiful blue eyes, tapped me on the shoulder. After explaining what I had come for I found out that I was indeed in the right place. She took me by the arm and stood beside me in one of the corners of the room. Her scent was like roses - meanwhile I was judging these people in their Jesus slippers; 'So this is what vegetarian people who like Yoga look like.' I felt such a distance between their world and mine. Obviously, they were not bothered by me being there in their sacred space. But, when some of them started hugging me, I wanted to leave. What had brought me to this place?

The millionaire who lost everything that mattered

It was 1999 and I had just resigned my executive job at the corporation where I had worked for more than 12 years. 'Bye bye beautiful car, cool titles, big salary and extravagant bonuses.

The good news though was that I had it all: I was the youngest divisional director of a very successful, prestigious, fast growing IT company in the Netherlands. I had become a millionaire. I had a beautiful wife and two lovely baby sons and, of course, a big country house.

When I came home and told my wife that I had resigned, she said to me: 'Michael, you know I cannot miss you, but, since you are never here, I want to give it a try.' Right away fear and stress came into my life. I hit rock bottom because I lost everything that I cared about; my wife, my kids, my job. Even our dog left me.

Listen to your coach

Feeling completely lost I found myself a coach who sent me to a breathing workshop, in order to learn to get my stress breathing, causing panic attacks, under control. So, there I was...

If it was not for my coach I would have left the happy, clappy, smelly, sweaty weird hippies immediately. Thank God it was only for two days and being a successful go-getter, I decided to stay to the end; 'So buckle up Mike.' After an exercise that seemed to me like a competition to see who had the saddest life story, we did an exercise where we had to look straight into each other's eyes. There was meditation music playing softly in the background and the hippy lady with the beautiful blue eyes recited a text about: 'What if it were into Jesus' eyes that you were looking?' Suddenly I got struck by an intense feeling that I couldn't pinpoint. It was so overwhelming. It was a feeling of oneness, love and happiness. It was then that I had my epiphany - I realized that we are all humans, we all have our dreams, our desires, our hopes and fears and no matter what we look like, we are all connected with each other.

And guess what, at the end of the workshop I could not stop hugging these wonderful freaks and I did not want to go back to my perfect but empty apartment, where I would be alone with my perfect but miserable self. That event really changed my life in an instant.

You are 100% responsible

Until then I had focussed on money, career, success and fast cars. It was me, myself and I, and according to my ex-wife, I was selfish, egocentric and arrogant. What about that? I must admit that I had not exactly been Mr. Wonderful in my marriage. I realized it's not about me. It's about being a loving and caring husband and father. Sometimes you only realize the value of things when you lose them. At some point my coach asked me: 'Michael, what went wrong, how did you get into these troubles?' So I came up with a whole list of reasons. My coach studied my list carefully and then spoke the magic words: 'Michael, I really don't understand why you are not on this list yourself! Do you want to be a victim or a victor?'

Victims are always complaining and blaming. The irresponsible person who lacks maturity believes finding the solutions to the problems of life is someone else's department. The moment you choose to be a victor and take responsibility you are in control and you claim back your power. You can change your circumstances.

What I have experienced is that success in life and business is never about money. It's about helping the people you lead and helping your customers to succeed. When they are happy, the money will follow. My paradigm shifted from getting to giving; giving value, service, attention and love.

The beauty of this mindset is that the universe works like a mirror: The more you give the more you will receive. This is one of the profound secrets that I am experiencing every day since my dramatic shift.

You get a second chance

Ever since my profound insights, I started my life all over again. To me it seemed that the universe had given me a second chance. I met the love of my life and we got married. My spiritual life really got a boost when I had some totally unexpected encounters with Jesus in my dreams and during several meditation sessions. With my wife I started helping young women with serious mental illness problems such as depression. Sadly, many of them have also been sexually abused. Mental health problems among women are on the rise worldwide. Nearly one in every five women experiences a common mental health disorder.

Besides that I have been looking for ways to help entrepreneurs succeed on their journey to success. Worldwide there are more than twenty million small and medium sized enterprises. Did you know that the majority are struggling with time, people, money, family and situations causing lots of stress and frustration? And that was exactly my home situation: My father was an entrepreneur and, besides the fact he was never at home, I always felt his desperation, fear, loneliness and frustration. So, I recognize the pain.

Make a contribution

Looking back, my life is more balanced and harmonious now: My spiritual foundation has its roots in gratitude and giving. My business is about supporting my wife in helping young, traumatized and depressed women recover and find new ways to pick up their broken lives and coaching business owners and executives to get their broken business going again. What I found out is that in every situation it´s about leveraging what you already have. In more than 90% of all situations with business people, the focus is on uncovering their hidden potential, talents, knowledge, ideas, concepts and skills. The majority of businesses are richer (in resources) than they think. The same goes for the young women. They need help to overcome their issues regarding trust, lack of confidence, self-esteem and fears such as rejection. They all have far more strength, courage, love and power than they think.

We only have to find out how we can help them to tap into their own resources.

We are all surrounded by people we can learn from, but sometimes it is so obvious we don´t even see it ourselves. We take people and things for granted and we are not aware of the real value. My first coach helped me to realize that by encouraging me to take full responsibility for my actions and my own life. The experience with the weird hippy people was a spiritual awakening -becoming truly aware that it´s not about me, but about we. And from that perspective: What is your unique gift to this world? What are you blessed with that you can offer to others as a blessing?

I realize that I have it all again, but this time 'having it all' has shifted to a different and deeper level of meaning and understanding. It really does not matter how many times in life you stumble and fall or fail as long as you are able to get up again, wipe off the dust and move on. When we are connected to our inner source of strength and are willing to learn and grow we can eventually become the person we need to be in order to succeed in life. Having a great coach really can help you to succeed faster, by the way. Many people ask me: 'Well Michael, great story but what about the money? Can money buy happiness?' 'I actually don´t think so, but having lots of money surely helps…'

About the Author

Michael Knulst (Netherlands) is an executive coach and a business strategist specialising in Innovation and Sales. He loves building businesses and taking them to the next level. His company Organizational Wealth can take your business from start-up to scale-up. During his career Michael has started up eight new companies, of which three have grown into multi-million-dollar businesses, two were lost due to bankruptcy and three were sold. So you might say he is a seasoned entrepreneur. Nowadays, he owns a consulting company, a software company and with his wife Carola he runs a mental healthcare institute. Michael is passionate about inspiring and empowering entrepreneurs to give their best selves in order to have successful businesses and fulfilled lives.

I Was A Writer Even Before I Knew I Could Write
Josien Frinking

When I was five years old, I placed a small table and a chair on my bedroom's balcony, I grabbed a pen and paper, and I sat myself down. I was ready to write. I wanted to share my stories with the world. I wanted to be seen by the people walking by, wishing for everybody to look up and say: 'Look at that little girl. She is only five years old and she writes the most beautiful stories!' As little gems, they were hidden inside of me, waiting for life to reveal them one at a time. And although I hadn't learned the skill yet - which drove me mad - I knew I was a writer even before I could write.

I asked my mom to help me write my first words: 'fountain pen'. Not just 'pen', 'fountain pen'. For some reason, this was oh-so important to me. I was so proud for writing such a big word, but I remember misspelling the word in class, which made me feel I wasn't good enough of a writer. And truthfully, no one explained to me that making an error wasn't the same as failing at it.

My two older brothers taught me a lot, like how to repair my bike. They would tease me for being a girl and dumb, which made me feel inadequate. I loved singing and dancing and performing. My grandmother taught us songs and plays, which we presented to our audience, the family. My brothers disliked performing to such an extent that they made me tell my grandmother we didn't want to do it anymore. I didn't want to at first because I loved performing, but they forced me and I gave in. Bummer for me. It wasn't until I was an adult that it really sunk in how much it had become my nature to put other people's needs before my own, neglecting the desire to follow my own dreams. Instead, I did what others expected of me. I adjusted and adapted. And I suffered in silence. A well-known drama teacher once told me that he just loved that ring of sadness around the iris of my eyes. It was part of a much deeper wound of not feeling wanted or loved.

Deserved to be loved

I grew up in a somewhat elitist and wealthy environment. We lived in a big villa in a small town where both my parents had successful careers. We grew up with a nanny, I attended private school, and I loved horseback riding and ballet. I also played the piano, and my wardrobe was filled with designer clothes. I had every reason to grow up happy and I was happy... as long as I was out of the house. Home was not a safe haven; it wasn't a loving and kind environment. My so-called successful parents were fighting non-stop (although they'd call it 'discussing life', which wasn't the case). It was violent and scary. I guess it was their way of dealing with life.

My father was of the dominant type and there wasn't much room for communication. He could turn aggressive on the spot for no reason. And he would lash out or beat and slap me to the extent that I would wet myself weekly out of fear for him. I don't know if I hated him or feared him most. He also touched me in ways a father shouldn't touch his daughter. To this day, I have trust issues with men because of it. My mother patronised the violence instead of protecting me, saying I was to blame. I caused trouble for her, she said. It was her survival tactic, her way of coping with family life. But instead of feeling safe and wanted and loved, it made me feel unsafe and ugly. And dirty.

As a child, I broke my head over whether my parents were truly my parents. In my mind, they couldn't be. My 'real' parents were loving and kind, and the day would come where they would find me and take me home with them. As an adult, I cried for this lonely and hurt little girl I once was.

At the age of 32, my father hit me one last time. His signet ring gave me a black eye. My mother hushed me to stop crying because it wasn't all that bad, but the doctor who examined me the next day was shocked, and he arranged for me to get help.

It took me a few years of therapy and healing to deal with the level of mistreatment. I had allowed anger and stress to build up inside of me. For so long, I had longed for the love and acceptance of my parents. I had done anything and everything to be good enough of a daughter to them; one who deserved to be loved. My parents had forcefully overstepped my boundaries. And I had started to do the same. I had started to mistreat myself, as well. I needed to learn how to create healthy boundaries for myself and those around me.

Accepting our gifts

I am not an exception to the rule when it comes to domestic violence and having low self-esteem as a result. 95% of us human beings have experienced some form of childhood trauma. That is sad. It explains why so many people are stressed, depressed, aggressive, and violent. It's old pain and neglect we haven't dealt with. I see it as our own task in life to unleash ourselves from our childhood layers and find our true authentic selves. To find our true heart's desire. I am the result of my upbringing, as my parents where the result of their upbringing. They didn't have the awareness of what they were doing, they were simply reacting and trying to minimise their pain. Not in a very elegant way, though.

Understanding how our mind and system operates has stopped me from blaming my parents. It has freed me from punishing myself for the way they have treated me. For how they used me. As... I used them. Without this path of upbringing I would have had only flowers and birds to write about. Now I have depth: hurt. Pain. Forgiveness. Great ingredients for a writer. It has unlocked the gems inside of me.

I consider myself lucky because God gave me a whole bunch of talents. He gave me survival techniques to sharpen my strength so that I am able to share these talents. I needed to be strong enough to develop perseverance, and I have. I am like bamboo: I bounce with the wind and I bounce back again to my oh-so strong center. I will never ever break because I understand life to the extent that life needs to be understood. God gives us gifts. We are not in the position to decide which gifts we accept and which we decline. We can dump unwanted gifts in the dumpster, they will not disappear. Instead, we drag the dumpster along with us in our lives until it pops open like a stinky jack-in-a-box. And this usually happens at very inconvenient occasions in life.

We have to accept all gifts we receive and deal with them. The fun gifts, the horrible gifts, the pretty gifts, and the ugly ones as well. Sadly, my youngest brother took his own life, which was a horrible gift. But the eternal soul connection that arose because of it was the greatest gift. Our connection is stronger than we have ever had in life.

I got beaten and abused in life to be able to understand pain and love. My heart was crushed because my gems needed to be released. It hurts. Life is not about happy clapping, this is not our learning curve. Life is about growing. And it comes with growing pains. Pain of regret. Pain of discipline. We tend to think we need to avoid pain, but this is so untrue. Pain is a sign of breaking free and it is supposed to hurt. I hope I have understood most of God's gifts. The bad, the ugly, and the beauty, too. Fearing my father has enabled me to sense people's energy. I have developed a helicopter view because of it where I can zoom in into detail and zoom out and see the bigger picture. This is talent and skill. It has made me an excellent strategist and business organiser. I use this tool in helping entrepreneurs and professionals get clarity on their business opportunities.

I have transformed my mother's critique (and sense for quality) into aiming for high quality for my clients, not settling for less than the best. My ability to chameleonise has given me a skill to understand customer needs, to read between the so-called lines. Life has given me survival tactics that have become my USP in business. It has made me a talented professional and I have been called a brilliant strategist and innovator, for which I am very grateful.

My early life has been based on pain and stress, which has resulted in wanting to work only with people who have pure intentions; people whose aim is to be happy and to do good to the world and each other. I have worked with many entrepreneurs who were stuck searching for their business' heart line. Business is about making a profit, yet most people lose their core values in the process. I get them back on track. I really turn people inside out if I have to! I want to know what makes them tick. We then make a plan for the future.

But there will also come a day when I am done with work and helping others. And when that time comes, I will take a seat on my bedroom's balcony. I will take my fountain pen and write my full life story. Until then, I am too busy living it.

About the Author

Josien Frinking (Netherlands) is a business organiser and entrepreneur. She is called a brilliant strategist and innovator, helping companies find their heart line and business purpose as a solid base for growth. Over the years, Josien has built, ran and successfully sold three companies. She is also a writer of two books. Josien speaks five languages and has lived and worked in the USA, Peru, France and on the Spanish island of Ibiza.

Standing Up For Your Ideals
Franca Gribnau

'How about the mystery of a unicorn? One of the most amazing, magical and graceful fantasy creatures you can imagine, living in secret places, full of colour and sparkle. Take some of that sparkle with you and enlighten the life of yourself and others.'

To be honest, I love such a fairytale world, filled with fantasy and dreams. As a little girl, I loved to read books. I would happily just fly away to these colourful places. But a colourful life doesn't have to be in your imagination only, though. What does this mean? In my belief, a colourful life is about living your life your way, choosing the direction that attracts you the most and that fits with who you are.

I hope to inspire you from a period I was an event manager, organising workshops for professionals in between jobs. The organisation I worked for was all about proactive networking and having a positive mindset, for instance, presenting themes like job marketing, personal leadership, and empowerment. Regularly, I was touched by the input and the stories of the workshop participants. It was the reason I committed to this volunteer job in the first place:

the impact and the power of a joined effort. When job loss or another life changing situation catches you off guard, you show character by how you handle the situation.

I was in the right spot to colour my agenda. Besides the pleasure of organising events and collaborating with inspiring coaches and trainers, it inspired me as a person. I experienced how important it is to be compassionate and became more aware of what people have to go through in life. I learnt not to judge so easily. Instead, I listened, inspired others by sharing tools and practical advice, and helped them create new perspectives. It's important to keep an open mind. It takes guts and commitment to find a new job, especially for the more experienced senior professionals in the job market. We all need new chances in life.

Higher-level questions

It is amazing how helping others often means growing as a person yourself. You get to know what makes you tick. I was in the middle of a career move myself and taking a course in entrepreneurship when this piece of advice struck a chord: reflect on your roadmap to success and take charge.

Of course, I was wondering how to get there. From all the methods I researched, these 'higher-level questions' impressed me the most: for who do you want to be of meaning? What value do you add to the life of yourself and others? How do you make a difference? How did you come so far and what do you need to 'rise and shine'?

Not the easiest questions, I know. They are about defining your DNA and your personal satisfaction. To me they were eye opening, showing me what really matters and what takes most of my focus. It's also about talents, strengths, weaknesses, and finding my favourite workplaces. My mindset switched. I am now living my life and making choices more consciously than ever. In my opinion, this is the key to bringing colour into your life. Let me share a part of my story with you.

As the little girl with her fantasy books, my life started in the east of the Netherlands. I grew up in a well-educated family, the eldest of two brothers and a sister. I loved creating a world of wonders of my own just by reading, crafting, and acting like 'mama junior' at home. In my childhood I got away with it. Duty called. We were raised to be responsible people with ambitions to make the world a better place. My mother was a medical analyst who later ran the household. Thanks to my father, managerial advice was always close by. He was a medical specialist and member of the board of directors of an academic healthcare centre for many years, the living example of 'being of service'. I am still grateful for that and I admire him for it. Above all, he taught us to have faith in people and in life. Work for it, learn, and grow. Just give it a try. In modern terms, it seems equivalent to the growth mindset, which is all about exploring your potential; the cycle of challenge, processing, focussing, learning, and growth.

Backbone

That was my cue. Throughout my life, I have constantly challenged myself to find a new purpose. I read management and leadership books. Even when on holiday, the bookstore was one of my favourite places. Although being laughed at sometimes, it intrigued me how vision, design, style, and photography are presented in other countries.

Then not so long ago, I 'released' myself from further digging. I realised that my purpose has always been there! My drive involves three C's: connecting, creativity, and communication. In addition, I have these ideals to go along with. For a long time, I thought it made me different; that it was a weak spot in the business world, me and my uplifting quotes, happiness magazines, and sensitivity to animal welfare.

I developed my backbone and I am thankful for my growing pains and lessons learnt. I now accept that I need a higher theme to inspire and motivate myself as it gives me something to strive for. Inspired and motivated, I contributed to making an impact in education, sustainability, and healthy and safe surroundings. It is rewarding to work on awareness and to create connection and commitment. Ambitious goals are being set at the larger (inter)national organisations where I have the opportunity to influence the bigger picture and make a difference. I believe that there is much to gain in respecting and managing differences, in crossing boundaries and turning them into synergy. Surprisingly enough, the modern era is now more on my side. Sustainability, value and meaning has a space within business where communication longs for emotion, client experience, and colourful stories. In my opinion, this will lead to a more balanced way of business in the future. I am happy to join in.

Colouring your life

I believe in the power of creation. There is an energy and flow that come from experimenting and exploring new ideas. It broadens the horizon, which I know from working in an international workplace. Through many years of taking art classes and creating my own art pieces in my spare time, I learned by experience that the challenge is not in the creation itself, although it may produce an absolute masterpiece. The creation is in the process, in creative thinking, collaboration, and the energy boost that comes with making a change or finding a brand-new solution. It can come about simply by looking at a situation from a different angle or seeing a bigger picture. In my opinion, the same goes for your professional life.

I am fascinated by human stories, love for animals, colours and contrasts. The combination of strength and vulnerability intrigues me time after time. For example, what lies beneath the special bond between people and animals? Or threats, such as endangered species? I am in awe of the often-unspoken emotions that it elicits in humans and curious about the progress still to be made. For instance, where social responsibility and protecting wildlife are concerned.

Colouring your life means standing up for your ideals. You have to earn your worth! I think my greatest challenge so far was to go for it just like that and cross those boundaries that I feared. It is the only way to live your life the best way you can. In my belief, the meaning of life is greatly defined by the value you add to it yourself. I found my practice along the way. I still treasure my fantasy sparkles, but with vision, as a grown-up does. Nowadays, to ensure I am staying on the right path, I regularly reflect on my ambitions. I challenge myself by picking new goals or ideas. It works! My professional ambition is to continue helping people and companies with their organisational and communication issues. I love to think ahead and work on new ideas, coordinate, and organise projects. And I will carry on pursuing my special interest in creativity and art.

I hope you find your roadmap or that you're well on your way. Make sure you have special things to contribute and look forward to. My personal inspiration: don't forget to imagine regularly, what you give attention to grows. Pick your goals and live up to them.

About the Author

Franca Gribnau (Netherlands) is an organisational and communications professional. She worked on communication projects and coordinated teams for many years. Fascinated by human stories, she has a love for animals and nature, and is passionate about safe and sustainable surroundings. Franca strives to make a difference by bringing more connection, colour and creativity to work and life.

Challenge Yourself Every Day
Gerjanne Scheffel

Think from the action mode. Apparently, this is necessary. Typical me… full time managing everything, kids, family, work. I observe. I see that men, without thinking too much about it, attack and even right after they have been beaten are ready for the next challenge.

I see that women have a tendency to withdraw. The feeling of inadequacy dominates. There's a voice in their head: 'Who don't you think you are?' and 'Don't have any illusions?' Similarly, there is a feeling that the right competencies are lacking. But can that really be true? I look at myself and decide to develop into a better version of myself. The best. The very best.

In my elementary school classes there were far more boys than girls. I often played the rough games with the boys. I enjoyed the action, the freedom and the unprecedented possibilities in those games. Looking back, I realize that this has had a crucial influence on my actions and the choices I made in life – choices I look back on with satisfaction to this day.

My first independent steps

My parents encouraged entrepreneurship. When I was six, I sold homemade cards and little figurines made from plaster. From the proceeds I bought nice things for my room and jewellery, or I saved the money. When I was twelve, I assisted a woman to make flower arrangements and selling them at markets. This was my first introduction to commerce. I became a staff member in a flower shop where I gave workshops on floral arrangement and I created wedding bouquets. This was preceded by an extensive exchange of ideas with the bridal couple; I learned to translate customer wishes and requirements into a product. I bought the fresh flowers I needed right from the auction. The colours and fragrances of flowers and the natural beauty of the seasons have always made me happy. These are a genuine source of inspiration and creativity.

I was born in a small picturesque village in the agricultural heart of the Netherlands where spotted cows dominate the landscape. I was the second child and first daughter in a family of four children, with ever-roaming chickens, dogs with wagging tails and affectionate cats. From a very young age I cycled with my brother or sister to the kindergarten, five kilometres away.

My independent assignments during my high school years initially came from a different angle. As a seventeen-year-old, I sent holiday photos to modelling agencies and was soon invited to do modelling work, photo shoots and TV jobs. However, the waiting periods and uncertainty surrounding follow-up assignments led me to enroll in a bachelor's programme in Education & Management after finishing high school.

The unknown on the other side of the world

In the last year of my bachelor's studies, I travelled to Japan with a fellow student to teach for four months, sponsored by a large multinational. In Japan we acted as ambassadors for this company. We taught at schools and worked in companies in exchange for a room and dinner. In this way, our trip and accommodations were largely paid for by the schools and companies we worked for. The new places, rituals and people we met inspired me enormously. The idea that anything was possible in this 24-hour economy made me think about the many opportunities this situation created. Our Western fixed patterns and customs were turned around 360 degrees here. As a result, I started considering this and merging the thought patterns of the West with the Eastern customs – from the combination of the busy streets with neon lighting in Tokyo to the relaxing bamboo forests on the outskirts of the city. Searching for balance between all stimuli is a challenge in every continent, but it's certainly possible. After returning to the Netherlands, I took up a traineeship at a large bank and then worked for two years in the corporate sector. But independent entrepreneurship was calling me. I started my own consultancy company, 'Finanze', with the big banks as my clients. As a compliance advisor, financing analyst, risk manager and interim manager, I help banking organizations become future-proof.

As an entrepreneur, I discovered that you must always have a knowledge advantage to be (and remain) of added value. I decided to attend the Dutch private university Nyenrode. Upon signing up, I discovered that I had too little knowledge of mathematics, so I had to quickly get myself to a sufficient level. My friend turned out to be a mathematics whiz and helped me through this and eventually – after an intensive catch-up effort – I could begin studying for a Master's degree in Business Administration and Management. The classes were held on Friday evenings and Saturday mornings, and during the week I continued working full-time. It was a tough time but the combination of working and studying with others also gave me a lot of energy and the drive to get better every day. Subjects such as Human Resources, Marketing, Ethics, Business Spirituality and Supply Change Management were completely new to me. Learning new things in a short time ensures that you look at the world objectively and are open to the new and unknown. After a few weeks, the unknown becomes known and enriches your life with a lot of new knowledge. Once you realize that, you'll have more confidence because you'll see that when you really try hard to achieve something, you succeed. No matter what it is. If your drive is strong enough, then you go for it.

Small talk

I have been working for banks for more than eight years now with my consultancy firm. Working at a large organization gives me the feeling that I am 'switched on'. Every day I meet new people and I have small talk at the coffee machine. I am interested in the story of how people shape their lives and what they do outside of work to recharge their batteries for the next day. As a risk manager, I manage the common risks in the field of corporate finance and loans. I look at the various aspects of the organization and where the biggest business risks are. My entrepreneurship skills ensure that I can quickly make an assessment whether a deal can be financed or not. I also occasionally have an audit or compliance role to check whether the business cases comply with laws, regulations and the policy of the organization. Occasionally I also give training courses on finance, risk & control and compliance. And despite the heavy material, the small talk remains very valuable to me. I once read that if you are open to new things, you become so much richer in experience and knowledge. That is why I have decided that every day I will speak briefly to someone I do not know.

Mrs. Fair

After my short-lived modelling career, the fashion world continued to beckon me. Together with a number of seamstresses, I run the clothing label 'Mrs. Fair'. This is a sustainable, ecological and fair-trade brand offering dresses for women and girls which are designed and made in the Netherlands. The children's clothing is produced under the brand name 'Little Miss'. The experienced seamstresses whom I have hired produce the clothing and work as trainers. They train women who have ended up on the edge of society in one way or another, from (former) prostitutes to people living on public assistance. By helping these women to rebuild their self-esteem and teaching them something new, I want to offer a new perspective. Mrs. Fair is for sale online and soon I want to open a 'brick and mortar' store.

Besides doing business, I find it important to have a supervisory function in an organization that adds value to society. For over five years, I have been a member of the Supervisory Board (Finance Committee) of the non-profit organization Mission Aviation Fellowship (MAF). MAF's mission is to ensure that nobody is unreachable. With 130 airplanes and modern communication tools, MAF ensures that people in the most remote areas can be reached for help and evangelism. Every five minutes a plane takes off somewhere to help people in need. It gives me great satisfaction to use my time, knowledge and (financial) expertise for this organization and the people who have left certainty behind to follow their mission.

Challenge yourself every day and be confident

I have always appreciated the beautiful statement of Eleanor Roosevelt: 'Do one thing every day that scares you'. My most important value is sharing the gifts and opportunities that I have received. Every day. Everyone is here on earth with their own task and it is up to everyone to do that task as well as possible. That task can change at different times but as long as my energy remains high, I trust it is the right one for the moment.

And certainly, as a woman in a business world dominated by men, do not let yourself get pushed to the side but take advantage of your opportunities. Search for the difficult challenges in your life. Go out, find an adventure, get to know people, laugh and keep an open attitude. Look around and enjoy all the beauty that comes your way. And where this leads you, you'll find out. What really matters is thinking about possibilities and making every day a bit better, more beautiful and being there for each other. Together with my husband, three daughters and two cats, I enjoy every day and live with gratitude. It often means working very hard, but after that it is also extra enjoyment of the success that we have achieved.

Through all the steps in my life, I have felt the presence of God. In my teens, He was a little more in the background because I was mainly discovering myself. During and after my Japan trip, I noticed that I cannot do without God. Every day He makes sure that there is once again light and the sun will shine again. Knowing that He is there and taking care of you, you can take on the whole world and face the new day with a smile.

About the Author

Gerjanne Scheffel (Netherlands) owns the financial consultancy firm Finanze. She acts as a risk manager, compliance advisor, financing analyst and interim manager. Gerjanne is married and has three daughters.

Too Focused To Give Up
Joy Onyesoh

As a young woman growing up, I had dreams of my future and, even though I had no clarity of purpose, I was convinced that I had a calling to do much more with my life than be self-centered. Struggling through life experiences, I sometimes forgot my reason or purpose and I did, indeed, live selfishly at times, but my conviction in my life's purpose kept bringing me back on the right track.

I tried many types of businesses - from merchandising to production to consulting - until I found my true purpose to help people, especially women, find their life's purpose and to inspire them to be the best version of themselves. I must confess that at some point, I felt like throwing in the towel and just flowing with the crowd. I will share with you three major elements that kept me going despite all odds. These are: redefining my meaning of failure and goals, consistency, and passion.

Redefining failure and goal

I discovered that, at times, we are limited by fear of failure fueled by society's pressure and judgment. I remember a period in my life when I couldn't identity who I was because I was motivated by the fear of failure and the judgment of others. This made me more of a people pleaser rather than trying to interrogate issues and forming my own opinions based on my reality and facts. I was careful not to step on others' toes, probably because I had a history of being misunderstood. I resigned myself to hiding my true self and flowing with the crowd so I wouldn't be noticed. I was afraid of letting my light shine brightly for all to see.

When I had my daughter and I was faced with her medical conditions, it was time to confront my fears after living in denial for too long. Can you relate to this? It may be denial in business or in personal situations. I was often scared of confronting reality because I was not ready to deal with the truth. It dawned on me that running away would not help my issues at all. Instead, I was constantly frightened and often at crossroads. Today I can take a walk down memory lane and laugh at some of the decisions that I made in the past, but I don't beat myself up about it. I now know that those where the best decisions that I could have made at that point in time.

Dealing with my daughter's medical situation built my resilience and changed my values. I learnt to redefine meanings and one of the meanings that I redefined was that of failure. I started seeing failures as opportunities for growing, learning and building my resilience. This, in turn, helped in shaping my goals. I further understood that my identity was constantly evolving because of my continuous interaction with people and situations. This meant that I had to constantly reflect on my core values, my goals, and myself. This process helped me in building my business as it is today; I don't take for granted the need for regularly evaluating processes and structures with the view of developing the best fit in the current situation. My early days of self-discovery are important building blocks to the person that I am today.

I learnt that my personal development was fundamental to building a solid business and personal brand. I don't take for granted the need to constantly invest in myself as this gives a high yield at the end of the day.

Consistency

One element of building a successful personal or business brand is consistency, which is the ability to be disciplined and focused in pushing towards your goals. It is important that your goals are measurable and that you are held accountable for achieving them. Your passion ignites your consistency. Some years back, when I was starting out and trying my hands in different types of endeavors while trying to find my calling, I was jumping around from business to business. I lacked the patience to actually grow the business. I had no system in place for evaluating and measuring the impact of what I was doing. I was going with my gut feelings and, while I am not discrediting the value of that, I eventually came to realise that it is important to have some clarity on the expected results as this makes you more committed to being disciplined and consistent.

I remember one incident very clearly as it marked a turning point in the way I organised my business and invested in myself. It was the failure of a training consultancy that I had secured. I was more focused on the profits that I would make rather than the services that I would be providing. Of course, during the whole process, I didn't feel this deep sense of satisfaction and I didn't give my best. I overlooked a number of little details and the business came crashing. Not only did it crash! I lost a lot of money and I had to repay some of the vendors whom I had contracted. That was my wake-up call. I was forced to spend time on self-reflection, trying to understand myself at that point and really defining what my priority was. The process broke me, but I came through it remolded and with a strong clarity of purpose. I can, therefore, say that passion, clarity of purpose, defined goals, accountability, and a mechanism for evaluating your progress ignites and ensures consistency.

Passion

I love watching my first son eat. He prefers to make his own meals and I am drawn to the care and confidence he exhibits while preparing his meal. However, watching him eat the meal is usually the icing on the cake. He is never in a hurry. He takes his time, concentrating on each bite. Watching him, you'll be convinced that the meal he is eating is the best meal he's ever had. You will be tempted to ask for a bite of whatever he is having. And that's the difference passion brings to a process. It lights up the process you engage in and convicts those who come across your pathway. When you are passionate about your goals, you seek ways to help you accomplish your goals and you enjoy the journey. I said earlier that personal development is fundamental to building a successful business, and I mean this in every sense of the word. As an individual, you are a project and it's your individual project that drives your business. There are certain skillsets that you need to acquire as an individual along the way that facilitate your business.

I have a passion for life and for putting a smile on people's faces. I love to be of service and to add value to others' lives. How did I get convinced of this? It took failing forward several times, getting up, and dusting myself off; it took a deep conviction that I had more to offer and more to get out of life.

My passion for life and my commitment to achieving my goals made me determined to stand out from the crowd. The experience of caring and nurturing a daughter with special needs helped me to rediscover my calling, overcome fear, and gain true clarity of my life's journey. I remember staying awake at night during the times I was going through my depression and denial stage and indulging in all sort of negative self-talk. Life lost a lot of its meaning for me, until I got to my turning point. Just as my son eats his meals with gusto and passion, I turned to the Bible and began to build a personal relationship with God. I did this with so much passion! Slowly but consistently, I gained inner courage; my resilience grew with each fracture and healing process that I went through with my daughter. I resolved that I would create opportunities for her and we would not feel sorry for ourselves. I took comfort in the words of the Lord that His gift adds no sorrow but gives joy divine.

My life took on new meaning. I decided to help women find and use their voices, which started out gradually as I was learning from my day-to-day experience caring for my daughter. I took on a new set of eyes and I could see opportunities for holding and helping hands. I was also building my experience and expertise. I knew it was time to start investing in myself in terms of enhancing and honing my skills so that I can be of service to more women. My years of service added to my years of building myself as a credible brand. My primary objective was to be of service, but I grew my brand to a point where I could be of service to different sub-groups of people and get paid for doing what I love most. I had to categorise services that are pro bono and those that I would collect payment for.

It's not been an easy road, but I am certainly living the life of my dreams. I look back at all the pathways that I have taken over the years and I do not have any regrets. I have redefined the meaning of most of the incidents in my past and they are my building blocks and my inspiration to be the best version of myself. I can proudly say that I am too focused to give up.

About the Author

Joy Ada Onyesoh (Nigeria) is the President and Founder of Joy Onyesoh Foundation, President of the Women's International League for Peace and Freedom Nigeria and International Vice President for the Women's International League for Peace and Freedom. Joy is an inspirational speaker, published author and life coach. Her slogan is 'Too focused to give up' and this drives her passion in making a difference in the lives of others. She is a passionate, self-motivated individual with a zeal to succeed, having excellent organizational and interpersonal skills. Joy's purpose is to inspire others to find their life's purpose and live an impactful life. She creates opportunities for women and girls to find and own their voice.

Who Are You Working For?
Angélique Monballieu

I started to work for myself when I was 52 years of age. Seven children, seven grandchildren, a fantastic family, and yet I always loved working. People didn't understand. For thirty years I worked for someone else's dream, not for my own, but I always loved what I did so I didn't realise it. Even the first fourteen years of being independent, I thought more about my clients than about myself. Suddenly, two years ago, my life changed. I had an appointment with my (biggest) client.

At this meeting, I was told that my services were no longer needed. Reality sunk in. Despite committing 200% to organising my clients' exhibitions, it was not enough. I went home and cried for days. In one moment, I had lost more than half of my income and I was not able to change that in the immediate future. I didn't know what I was going to do.

The decision

I decided to completely quit working in exhibitions, and that meant leaving behind working weekends, long days, and hurriedly building up and taking down stands... The first period of being 'unemployed in exhibitions' was in the summertime (read no-exhibition time). I started some projects that I could do from my office at home. With my husband working in export and often away from home, and with two children still at home, it was easy to earn money. But I didn't feel very happy.

After the summer, the exhibition season started up again and I went visiting. That's when I first doubted my decision to leave it all behind. Communicating with people, realising an exhibition project, being able to build a stand with a team in a few days, networking, and creating an atmosphere where everybody felt happy and, most of all, I felt happy, too. I missed it all.

At 52 years, I still had fifteen years of my working life ahead of me. My youngest children would leave home in a few years to study and have their own families. My husband would be away, and I would be at home working on projects for others to earn money. But my heart, my passion, and my enthusiasm for exhibitions would still be there without anything being done about it. I decided to look out for companies who participated in exhibitions and were looking for some helping hands. But it was difficult. I realised that either the company wanted help but had no money, or the company had money but also a marketing department and they didn't want the help.

The opportunity

I felt disheartened, but I kept believing in my ability to earn money by working in exhibitions. In the meantime, I kept doing other projects to earn money. At the same time, because I had time, I continued to visit exhibitions. I started to notice that every exhibition had the same problems. Talking to exhibitors and talking to exhibition managers…they had the same demands, they had the same problems… both realising that they could do better, but didn't know how. Or they did know how, but they didn't listen to each other.

That's where I saw a gap. One of my biggest problems was that I did not realise my experience of being at exhibitions for more than twenty-five years had great value. For me it was normal to give people free advice about exhibitions, not realising that I was giving away money I could be earning for my family.

At the same time, I was developing my own skills by attending webinars and taking online courses. I started following a Belgian business coach and signed up for her online course. When the course was cancelled, I was given a choice: get my money back or meet her. I chose to meet her.

A fresh perspective

I drove all the way to the seaside, not knowing that it would change my life once more. We started talking about the things that were important to me. According to her, they weren't the right ones. When I started speaking about my dream of looking for another firm where I could organise their exhibitions, she looked at me and said, 'I would have paid someone to help me with exhibitions in my previous job, because I didn't know where to start.'

She asked me two questions. The first one: 'Ten years from now, would you want to get up in the middle of the night to build a stand?' The second question: 'What would you say if you could coach or advise entrepreneurs and firms wanting to participate in exhibitions?'

At first, I did not say much. Then I thought that in ten years, I would be over sixty. Already having problems with my neck and back, it would not be any better. And helping others was one of the things that I already did without asking for money. If I wanted to change for the years to come, I had to do it now. I did not sleep well that night, thinking about it over and over again. Realising that I could share my experience and be a small part of making the exhibition world turn the other way excited me. One exhibitor at a time, one exhibition at a time, I could make a difference.

A new dream

How I did not know, but yes, the idea was born. I also realised that it was the only way for me to be happy in my work for the years to come. It would take time to get there and I wouldn't be earning a lot of money at first. A problem to be solved. Would it be possible to combine my passion for exhibitions and earn money? It was strange realising that I would, for the first time in my working life, pursue my own dream and not someone else's. Using my energy for my own business, that was new for me. What if I could, for the first time in my life, create with my own passion, my own dream? It felt amazing. The start of a brand-new life.

'How would I do it?' was my biggest question. Believing in my dream was the first step, followed by a positive mindset and sharing my dream with plenty of people. What else was needed? Social media, Facebook, LinkedIn, and all new ways of communicating. Talking, communicating, calling people... networking.

Speaking to exhibition managers and hearing they had problems with their exhibitors because they started too late with their preparations, didn't think about what their goals were, or didn't follow the leads. Speaking to entrepreneurs that didn't participate because it was too expensive, too much work, they were uncertain about what exhibitions they would participate in, or they weren't convinced the results would pay off.

I realised that I had two different types of clients and I wanted to be able to connect them. What could I do to connect exhibitions with exhibitors? I started writing a book even though I never wrote before. I knew what I wanted to say, but I didn't know how to bring it across in a perfect way. Perfect was my problem. Telling it all was impossible! I had to share just enough that it had enough value in a way that everyone could understand.

The Exhibition Success Method

The 'Exhibition Success Method' was born, and it was the start of my book. In June of 2018, my book 'Exhibition Success' was launched in Dutch and will be released in French and English.

It took me a year to combine working on other projects to earn money with working on my dream to do what I love to do. It will take me months, even years, to achieve the goals that I still want to reach, but I feel that I've come home. I am where I want to be for the years to come in my working life. My bigger goal is to perfectly balance my professional and personal life and although I am not there yet, I am getting there! I've already decided to learn all I can about automation over the next few months. I want to do the things I love to do and help my clients at the same time.

The most important life lesson was that you have to think about yourself. I didn't forget that I have a family and friends, but for many, many years, I forgot myself without realising it. I thought I was happy, I felt happy. I have great children, I love my grandchildren, but I forgot about putting myself in first place.

Participating in this book is my way of giving you an opportunity to think about life. Are you doing what you most want to do? Are you happy? Is your life in balance? Or do you think more about what other people might think of you if you pursued your dreams? Don't wait as long as I did to love myself at the age of 52. Believe in what you want and start now!

About the Author

Angélique Monballieu (Belgium) is mother of seven children and a grandmother. She loves exhibitions and wants to share her experience with clients who want to participate at exhibitions and to help exhibitions managers improve their exhibitions by working with their exhibitors. Her clients describe her as dedicated, passionate, enthusiast, connected, open-minded, interesting and energetic.

From Victim To Leader
Tony Rekelhoff

My life is a labyrinth made up of several layers. For years, fears and learned beliefs clouded my self-image and future possibilities. My youth ended with a backpack full of experiences that a girl my age should not have been expected to carry. On my 25th birthday, I took control of my life...for myself and for my two-year old child. I gave myself permission to change. I took my optimistic character and went on a mission. No longer subject to fear, guilt, and the other negative emotions that were weighing me down, I learned to observe from the consciousness of a possibility thinker.

This change wasn't easy. What I experienced in the world as I was learning, it did not match my inner image. My reality was tinged with trouble and poverty despite my solution-focused personality. With time, my ability to see the solutions and not the problems helped me see that I was innovative. It opened me up to opportunities to learn and change my life. I no longer allowed the opinions of others to be more important than my own opinion. I stopped being obedient and adapting to the expectation of others.

I realised that if I continued to let my choices be determined by learned fears and assumptions, I would deprive myself of the opportunities to grow and develop in a way that is right for me. I parked my fears and took matters into my own hands. Many coping mechanisms were active in my brain, which were not always pleasant. They kept me from trusting myself and my ability to lead my life in a better direction. So there was work to be done. Giving up was not even an option for me. I believed in my dot on the horizon. I remained true to what I experienced deep inside of me. Sticking to my truth and integrity gave me the strength to continue. I put everything aside that I had ever heard and learned. I made new experiences and used the old ones where they served me. I found out that help is always available. This, and the conviction that life was meant to be different, gave me confidence and courage to go on. I learned that the value I give to my thoughts determine my life. They are a big part of how I experience my life. So much of my self-worth has been lost because I believed what was said to me. This clarity came only after renovating my mental network.

Observer of my own life

The money from my piggy bank was (without my permission) used by others, which gave me the belief that having and saving money was useless. Other people could take my money whenever they liked. Three times in my life I lost my house and all my belongings and I had to start over again. The first time was when my parents divorced, the second time because of a fire, and the third time because of my own divorce. The result was a mountain of debt and, again, I was in a hopeless situation. This desperation awakened the fighter in me. My child would have a mother to be proud of, not a mother who was a victim. I wanted to give him a better base and be a better example than I have had. My talents and abilities started working together.

Growing up, the negative opinions and assumptions in our home about other people confused me. How I experienced the people and my environment compared to what was said about them was totally different. All these assumptions, opinions and warnings, however well intended, made me doubt myself so I held back my opinions. I understood the world around me less and less, experiencing double messages. I adapted and started showing more and more acceptable behavior.

There were also assumptions about me. I felt decisions concerning me were already made and me saying 'no' would not make any sense. There was no listening to my opinion. If I had the courage to speak up, it would be followed by a whole discussion, or an instruction to do what was expected of me. I concluded that I had nothing to say about my own life. I stopped asking questions, there were no answers. I adjusted even further until something in me shut down. Loneliness was born. I became a servant because it was easier; less problems and resistance. I felt insecure and sad. Loneliness grew. Alone and closed down, I became an observer of my own life. All the words I had ever heard became my inner voice. Disapproving and always negative. I realised that the first thing I needed to do on my path to change was to change the lyrics playing in my head.

The perceived difference between our lives at home and the environment was huge and, at the same time, fascinating. This sparked my curiosity. How do others live? The desire grew. Born with an inquiring mind, this was exactly what I was going to do; investigate and learn.

Survival mechanisms

I had internal survival systems that I was not proud of so I made the most courageous decision of my life: 'I am going to change.' I decided my survival systems no longer determined my life. I, myself, was at the steering wheel of my life. I said thank you to my old systems and went looking for new ones.

Apparently, I was a victim. Or at least, that's how I was labeled. Although bad things happened to me, I never saw myself as a victim, though. After all, there were so many pleasant experiences, too. I also knew so many lovely people. But then a strange coping mechanism kicked in. Something in me started looking for proof of my victimhood. I crawled into the victim's skin. This gave me recognition and understanding. It brought relief. Apparently, I was rightly a victim. The people were right. Recognition and getting to understand my victimhood became a mission. My thoughts became more and more critical and negative towards myself, up to a point that I did not recognise myself anymore. I became dependent on getting understanding and recognition. A very turbulent and confusing time for me because, after all, I did not feel like a victim.

Yet I became one. By saying about myself, 'I am a victim', I determined how others saw me. I gave the other person permission to treat me as a victim. This pattern of 'it takes one to know one' helped me understand what victimhood entailed and the benefits of being a victim.

Other people labeled me as a victim and, therefore, expected certain behavior. If I did not show that behavior, they where confused. One day I went to see a psychologist. Because I did not live up to the picture he had of a victim, he could not do anything for me and we said goodbye. This experience again left me wondering what other people expected from me. It was totally different to what I expected from myself and from life. For a long time, I stayed in the corner of my victimhood. I had no substitute behavior, no other frame of reference.

Slowly, I understood that I had adopted the behavior of a victim. The moment I realised it was the moment that I could say goodbye to it. I had regained some of my true leadership. I experienced my inner self totally differently and again I decided to trust my feelings and follow my own guidance.

From childhood, I felt unseen and misunderstood. Still today I am surprised when I feel someone understands me on a deeper level. I am grateful to recieve this understanding and enjoy the feeling of it, but I no longer depend on it. The need to be understood was like as a drug. It was never enough.

When I discovered that a feeling of loneliness was underneath my need for wanting to be understood, I took care of it by surrounding myself with other people. I started to give help from the heart wherever I could do good. And I still do.

My lessons learned

- You are worthy to do your best for yourself.
- There is always a way out. You will find it step by step.
- Give yourself permission and your tomorrow will be different.
- Your value is greater than you realise. It is!
- Stay true to your strength, integrity, and leadership.
- Let go but never give up.
- Everything is temporary and in motion. You determine the direction.
- Show your unique self, be courageous.
- Stand up fully in the sun or in the rain. But stand up, make your life count.
- You know who you really are. You know your inner self. Support her (or him).
- Surround yourself with people who have a positive attitude and humor!

I am grateful for my talents, they give me a range of possibilities. I wish for you to live your life fully and happy. I know I do.

About the Author

Tony Rekelhoff (Netherlands) grew up in a working class familiy as the youngest of four daughters. She is intrigued by the power and possibilities of the brain. With her own coaching practice, Tony has helped many women making an impact within their business, family and personal lives. Tony confronts women about their self-esteem and strength and puts them in touch with their leadership, while discovering their true talents.

How A Little Girl Slayed Her Dragons
Anne Vrieze

Once upon a time, there was a little girl. She was ten years old and lived with her sister and her parents in the Netherlands, where they had finally settled after moving from country to country many times through the years. The girl always felt she didn't fit in. She was insecure about herself because of her red hair and freckles. At school, she felt sad because she was bullied by other kids. She was bullied for her red hair; they called her 'lighthouse'. She was bullied because she was tall; they asked her if it was cold up there. But most of all, they bullied her because she was the best in her class.

The little girl was surrounded by narrow-minded people living in her neighbourhood. If you held your head high, they would cut you down. Not being conscious of this, the little girl literally held her head high as the tallest of her class. Her red hair and intelligence made her an even bigger target. Often, she cried herself to sleep, desperate to find a solution for the bullying. That little girl was me. My story tells you how this insecure little girl became a successful online businesswoman.

My parents never stood up for me. Maybe because they were too busy with themselves, maybe they didn't feel the need to stand up for me, or maybe they didn't see what was really going on. I don't know. I didn't talk much with them about the bullying. My grandmother tried to cheer me up by telling me I had beautiful red hair and saying that my classmates were just jealous of it. Even that didn't help. Years later, at a reunion when I was in my thirties, some of my old classmates surprised me by saying they always thought I would be a director of a company and very successful. At the time, they didn't realize how close they were to the truth. Neither did I! But their words brought some much-needed healing and I was grateful for that.

Equality

At twelve, I went to high school in a nearby town along with my best friend. I was happy to leave all the bullies behind in my hometown. Meeting my new classmates brought me so much joy. They were all tall and intelligent, and one girl even expressed her relief that she wasn't the only tall girl in class. Instantly, my insecurity disappeared. School became a happy place and it didn't even bother me that I had to cycle ten miles every day to get there.

After graduating at eighteen, I studied social sciences at the University of Amsterdam. I made it all the way and I obtained my Master's degree in Orth Pedagogics, the science of children with a handicap. Volunteering for handicapped scouts was something I really enjoyed during my studies and even after. Why? I had to use my creativity to make them take part in the games we played at the scouts. What I didn't know back then was that because I was bullied at school, equality had become very important to me. I wanted to be treated equally and so I wanted others to be treated respectfully and equally as well.

After I obtained my Master's degree, I couldn't find work as a social scientist. It was in the 1980s and we were in the middle of an economic crisis. There were no jobs in social sciences and social work, so I started working as a secretary for employment agencies to make some money. Within a few years, I was working as an assistant for the Department of Social Services of the municipality where I was living. My manager thought I could grow to become a policy advisor and gave me work on the level of a staff member. Although I was happy with this new step in my career, I was still paid as an assistant. But not for long. I started growing more and more, and within two years, I became a well-paid policy advisor and project manager for the municipality's social services. After a while, I changed to another municipality where I could further my growth.

Enough!

After seventeen years of working for municipalities - I was 45 years old - I decided it was enough. I wanted to develop myself and I felt I couldn't do that in the small town where I was working. They were constantly restructuring, which became a distraction and took my focus away from what was most important to me: The people in the town and their happiness. I also needed the freedom to do what I wanted to do. I decided to start my own business in policy consultancy. From that moment on, I was able to focus on social policy and people.

In the meantime, I got married and had two children. When I decided to start my business, my daughter was sixteen years old and my son eleven. Now, ten years later, they also have their own businesses and I am very proud of them. The eldest has a business in innovation and communication. The youngest owns a business in the events branch. My husband is employed, and he feels safe in doing that.

I landed two assignments immediately after deciding to start my business, so I resigned from my job at the municipality. My business did very well and after eight months, I bought a new car for the first time in my life. This made me so proud. It wasn't an expensive car, but it was new and beautifully red. After working for three years as a consultant, I wanted to move to the next level. I started working with business coaches and I attended a business coaching program. At first, I didn't like it because it seemed so American, which is so much different from the Dutch culture. However, by the second day, I was dancing with the other participants and I loved it. After that, I followed several business coaching programs that allowed me to grow as a person and empowered me to grow my business.

Online solution

I had a setback in 2012 when I was struck by a hernia and could only work for one or two hours a day. This was a clear sign; I had to start thinking about other business models. I had plenty of time to think about it while I was lying on my bed, unable to work. Still I had no clue what I would do.

My inspiration came in 2014 when I started teaching courses on Dutch social law for civil servants of municipalities. I was freelancing for two training institutions, but it wasn't satisfying because these organizations wanted me to teach out-of-date content.

New laws were on their way in and I discovered that civil servants would need a set of new skills for the execution of these laws. They especially needed to learn to be more customer oriented. I had a vision of how to help civil servants adapt to these changes and I decided to follow this vision by starting a unique online academy. The courses I teach at my online academy emphasize creative thinking. I believe that when professionals ask their clients what they need and design a creative solution in response to this need, then they are treating them as their equals and creating happy clients.

By the end of 2014, I launched the first online courses and very soon they became a success. My business was growing fast! After three years, I was able to give up my consulting work completely and focus solely on my online education business. During this time, I had created a team around me and my business consisting of ten talented professionals, including a virtual assistant, three trainers, a marketing assistant, a Facebook and Google Ads marketer, and an account manager. My business had a list of 3.000 prospects and 150 to 200 students per year. In 2017, I became the Business Woman of the Year in my hometown because of my high revenue and social activities.

My lessons learned

- When I was a little girl, I didn't fit in. Now I have learned that you have to stand out in the crowd if you want to be successful.

- Put all your energy into working on your business. Focus on one business and as little products as you can to make money. Only if your energy flows in, the energy pours out.

- Creating a detailed business plan is not really necessary, but you do have to know where you want to go. Furthermore, you need to be focused and you need to be aware of your talents.

- Trust and let go. Use the Law of Attraction. You attract what you really need, and in a natural way, you don't attract what you don't need. So don't try to force business, just let it come.

- Find yourself a business coach who stimulates you and kicks your ass.

- Surround yourself with business friends who are on your level and start a mastermind group to empower each other.

- And last, but not least, stay curious. Look for innovation and new opportunities. If you don't challenge yourself, you will stand still and your business will drop dead.

About the Author

Anne Vrieze (Netherlands) is owner of WWZ Consultancy and WWZ Academy.

You Are Special
Carola van Berckel

Since childhood I longed for distant countries where I could experience adventure and escape the harsh reality of everyday life. I was a dreamer, a sensitive child and understood absolutely nothing about the world around me and often felt misunderstood. Around the animals, I felt safe and trusted and developed a bond that went beyond most friendships.

That's how I ended up in the world of horses. And because of my special ability to connect to them on a much deeper level, I can effortlessly communicate with these noble, free and sensitive animals.

I am known as a horse behaviour expert and equine coach and my work with horses has opened the way into the world for me. The dedication I have to them is focused on building relationships based on trust and understanding.

In the place where I grew up, we tend to go for security, to keep control. The danger of society we live in, however, is that people have expectations; we often follow the wrong paths for ourselves with the illusion that everything is feasible. In my neighbourhood most people were focused on performance and education, while I much more preferred to follow the butterflies.

Breaking out

I too felt compelled to fit into a straitjacket, to have to comply with the norms and values of the world, especially those held by the people around me. From the need to belong, to be seen and recognized for who I really am, I started to conform myself to my environment.

I started behaving like a chameleon. Doing exactly what was expected, depending on the situation, but deep inside I was unhappy. This is not as I had imagined my life, it was distressing me, I wanted to leave. The desire to be unleashed, to discover all my possibilities became stronger and eventually I was at a crossroad in my life. Would I be left with the old for fear of the new, or was my desire to break out of the invisible chains, that had held me prisoner for years, strong enough? Strong enough to take the dive into the deep, to a world that was totally unknown to me? I realized that it was time to take one of life's most important decisions. Little did I know that it would become the most significant one in my life.

At that point, where many people get stuck and dare not jump, but remain in quiet despair, continuing to lead their old safe lives and sometimes even becoming ill, I made other choices. I quit my job, sold my belongings and went abroad for an indefinite period of time. As a child I had the desire to swim with wild dolphins, the time seemed right. I started doing what I had experienced so many times in my dreams.

The people around me thought it was strange, but knowing I had to do this, only made me more determined. The desire for freedom – the search was stronger than my fears. What I was actually looking for was not even really clear to me, but there was no doubt in my mind that I wanted to get out of the current situation. To be free, without anyone else determining what I did or how I did it, neither feeling condemned nor judged.

With an open ticket in my pocket but without a plan, I went on an adventure. What I did not realize was that this journey was actually an escape and would bring about such a transformation in my life.

Journey of life

I landed from one adventure into another. Almost daily, I swam with wild dolphins, with whales, sharks, giant turtles and manta rays. I met several internationally known people, have been to places that most people only dream of and had deep spiritual experiences. In Hawaii I experienced the phenomenon of synchronicity first hand - accidents in disguise, that happen in every life and can give your life a radical turn. When I started to see the 'coincidences' on my journey, I ended up in a kind of flow. A wonderful and enthralling feeling. I kept on suddenly meeting people and being in the right place at the right time.

Letting go of my old life created room for new experiences. And I realized that if we say goodbye to things that no longer fit us, the space that is created will be filled with good things in our lives. For example, before I embarked on the journey of my life, I ended my relationship with the man I had lived with for many years. He was not 'Mr. Right'. Of course, I knew that for a long time, but yes, also here the pattern of holding on to what you have, kept me stubbornly stuck. While choosing adventure, freedom and happiness, I met the man of my life with whom I am now happily married. What I have also been able to experience is that if you dare to trust and you dare to surrender to life, the universe will take care of you. Perhaps it is not the fear of the unknown, but the fear of living that keeps us trapped.

My spiritual journey has enriched my life in a way that I could never have planned. The experiences and insights have helped me to discover myself again and with that I have embraced the gift of life. We can inspire others with what inspires us!

Appreciate the moment and happiness will follow. This is the lesson the animals taught me. They know no past or future and live only in the now. The moments when I chose to be, rather than to do, have brought me so much joy. During the encounters with the dolphins, beautiful metaphors were unfolding making a lasting impression. I was able to observe and study these beautiful mammals extensively. In that same period, I also met the great authority in this area, Joan Ocean and learned a lot from her. Dolphins live in harmony, love, friendship and freedom and enjoy every moment. We can learn a great deal from them. All we have is the moment that we now experience. You can create this moment and be totally present. If you become aware of it, if you can connect with creation, you are able to experience unity.

Unity

At a certain moment I knew I had to go back to the Netherlands, the place that once felt confining. Nature has arranged that so nicely; there is a time and place for everything. I have learned that freedom is only where there are boundaries. There can be no freedom in the absence of borders. And this freedom is deep inside, within everyone. So it is also with you.

The most beautiful breakthrough on Hawaii was the experience of unity, while swimming with the dolphins. At a given moment I felt like one with the dolphins, the ocean, the sounds, the multitude of colours and everything that was happening around me. It was a heavenly experience where time didn't exist.

Only much later did I realize that we are all connected to each other. Your pain is my pain and your happiness is my happiness. Yet we are all unique and special. If I am special, you are too. When I radiate, I invite you to shine and when I laugh, the world laughs with me.

Did you know that on Hawaii horses are considered the dolphins of the land? They see horses as dolphins on land because they have the same mission and they live in this moment. And that's how the circle completed for me. I often think back to that special time in Hawaii. The experience I had with the dolphins and all the beautiful people I have met and with whom I feel deeply connected.

My choice for life, the leap into the unknown, has become the journey of my life. A spiritual journey, like the erstwhile natives did to connect with their spirit. It has brought me where I am today, it has enriched me and also made me realize that wherever you go, you always take yourself with you.

I have made peace with myself and the most beautiful gift I have received is the connection with true self, with my authentic self. I hope that I have been able to inspire you with my story and that this may be your invitation to choose life. Because you are special. I pray for you to have wisdom, love and blessings.

About the Author

Carola van Berckel (Netherlands) is an expert in the fields of equestrian language, authentic behaviour and coaching. She has been travelling all over the world to train and inspire people into developing a better understanding, a deeper connection while bonding with the horses. As a life strategist she coaches and trains people in authentic leadership, intuitive decision making and intentional living. Carola is a born-again Christian whose mission is to inspire and empower women to break their chains and step into their greatness.

Abundance Is In Me
Cindy Vranken

'Look Cindy, you're almost there!' the porter said. And yes, some 25 metres ahead I caught a glimpse of a sign which read: Congratulations, you are now at Uhuru peak, Tanzania, 5895 m, Africa's highest point.

Applying any and all reserves I had left in me, I clambered towards the top of the Kilimanjaro like a woman possessed. As it's not very sensible to start running on a mere 77% oxygen level I heard cries of 'Pole, pole, Cindy!' ('Slowly, slowly, Cindy!') But I refused to let this influence me. Reaching the summit, I immediately collapsed, but was helped up by a couple of guides and let out a primal yell: 'Yesssss! I did it!' It was -15° Centigrade, I was dizzy, sick to the stomach and had a bursting headache. I was shaking like a leaf, but felt – literally – on top of the world: Invincible.

Nine months previously, I'd decided that I wanted to pursue a healthier lifestyle. I had wrestled with my weight and my body for what seemed like forever and suffered from the associated lack of energy and self-esteem.

Yet, I ran a successful business and I felt that in order to go to the next level I had to focus on improving my health.

Shortly after this resolve, I received a phone call from a business acquaintance who asked me if I wanted to join a group of entrepreneurs in tackling the Kilimanjaro for a worthy cause. Me: 'What exactly is the Kilimanjaro?' 'The highest mountain in Africa.' 'Oops, a mountain! But I'm afraid of heights and I've never climbed a mountain before. What about privacy up there? I want my own room en-suite...' I countered. 'Sorry, no bathrooms. We're sleeping in tents.' Six days without a shower! Never! My head said 'No'. My friends, family and clients said I was crazy. Still, my heart gave an immediate, wholehearted 'Yes'.

What if I reached the summit! This challenge would be an excellent incentive to achieve the healthy lifestyle I was looking for. I imagined myself at the top and felt the energy flow. This mountain would symbolise all of life's hard lessons that I'd been burdened with throughout my life. I could conquer my fears once and for all, and leave all my burdens at the summit. Then, I'd be able to lead my business through my inner strength. I accepted the challenge with fear in my heart.

So there I stood: at the summit, after months of intense preparation. It had been a roller coaster ride of falling down and getting up again. Of countless confrontations with myself. I'd known that doing it alone wasn't an option, so I'd hired a personal trainer who drew up a training schedule including interim targets. I'd sought help from a dietician and lost kilo's. Despite injuries to my Achilles tendon and calves, I refused to be beaten: I trained in a 4.500 meter altitude chamber twice a week and slept in an altitude tent the last month. Eventually, I knew that I had given all I could and, in the process, had actually already reached my goal of a healthier style of living!

Determined to grow

Taking up the challenge was something I'd done my entire life. I was born to a working class family and my parents, forgoing higher education, went out to work at sixteen. At home, arguments about money prevailed and I was taught that life is tough, that you have to work hard to earn a living and that I would never amount to much in life. The more I was told that I was a loser, the more I was determined to develop, to grow, to become the best at everything I attempted. I regularly fantasized about my future: I'd lead a successful business, motivate and inspire thousands of people from a podium, earn an astronomical salary and donate large sums to charity.

This growth mindset enabled me to conquer the mountain, just as much as it helped me to conquer life when it seemed to become unbearable. I know, from experience, that the hardest lessons in life are also the greatest gifts to yourself.

Take the unplanned pregnancy and the birth of my daughter Kimya, for example. When specialists told me she might remain in a persistent vegetative state, my entire world fell apart. I had never chosen to have children and now I had a handicapped child with an uncertain future to cope with just as I was starting to develop an amazing professional life for myself.

What I didn't realise, was that I was in survival mode. So intent on outward appearances: proving to everyone what a super woman I was, that I'd lost all touch with my inner self and my emotions. Until Kimya's birth, my head ruled all aspects of my life and I was at a loss to express my feelings, which ranged from anger to grief and guilt. Kimya literally woke me up, for which I will always be grateful to her. I embarked on a series of courses to address my personal and emotional development, step by step learning to trust my own heart, my inner guide.

Another of life's valuable lessons was my divorce. Splitting up with Kimya's father after sixteen years meant I lost absolutely everything: my job, my partner, my home, my friends and eventually myself. It was as if I didn't exist any longer. That was how paralysed I felt. I was in such a very dark place that even life didn't hold much meaning for me any longer. All that kept me from doing the inevitable, was my little girl. For months I cried, shedding all the emotions I'd kept bottled-up inside me throughout my life. Kimya regularly comforted me, putting an arm around me and telling me: 'It's okay mama.'

Now or never!

I was the only one who could turn this around, because I was the one who had created this situation. So I registered for a week-long course on transformational breathing. During that week, a miracle happened: I felt reborn, saw a future for myself, regained my self-confidence and, less than a month later, was given the job of a lifetime, organising international strategic collaborations for a software company. The job took me to New York, London and Paris. I was paid a top salary, and within months I'd set up a very successful partnership network for my employer. However, I worked 24/7, hardly had time for Kimya and knew I was heading for a burn-out if I continued in this way.

Secretly, I hoped I'd be fired and this happened just prior to my fortieth birthday. Two months earlier, I'd registered for a five-day course in Milan (Italy) to learn how to set up a business successfully. I'd always cherished this dream, but had been held back until then by my father's admonishing words that becoming your own boss was a risky business and that it paid off to opt for the security of working for someone else. In spite of my own employer refusing to let me have time off to go to Milan, I went anyway.

So this was it. It was now or never! I had dreams and no-one would take them from me. Despite my fear of failure or my anxiety about not having enough money, I followed my heart, taking a full nine months to prepare for the start-up of my own business in a fully committed and fully focused way. To everyone's surprise, my initial launch recouped a six-figure sum in its first month, allowing me to grow and attain the next level quickly. Now, I can honestly say that I'm leading the life I dreamed of: I choose when to work and who with, I have time for my daughter and my loved ones. I go abroad regularly and, more important, I enjoy and appreciate my success.

My basic principles

The last three years have been the most instructive of my life and, whether it's about becoming happy and fulfilled, or leading a successful business, or reaching the summit of Mount Kilimanjaro, there are a few basic principles that have helped me attain all these goals and that I would like to share with you.

- Always focus on what you want, not on what you don't want. Set your goal, draw-up a plan and keep it simple! So what is the easiest way to reach your goal? Commit yourself 200% to everything you do. However hard it gets, keep going and don't give up. Winners never quit and quitters never win.

- Listen to your inner voice. It always knows what's good for you. Challenge yourself constantly and set ambitious targets. You are capable of so much more than you think you are. Stretch your comfort zone and magic will happen.

- Surround yourself with positive, uplifting people who've already achieved what you are aiming to achieve. Look for a teacher, mentor or coach who believes in you and will inspire you to take the next step. Know you're not alone and you don't have to do it alone. Show courage in asking for help.

- You are the director of your own life and your own reality. Never allow circumstances or someone else to take over this directing role. Is life difficult and hard at this moment, then discover your thoughts and convictions focus on the positive thoughts and on what you want and change will happen fast.

- You are big, so dream big! It is your responsibility to help as many people as you can with your talent. For years, I was told I was a loser. I believed this until I realised that this was not my reality. I am worthy and, ever since I started believing this, miracles happen.

I was addicted to drama and was happy being a victim. Until I realised that everything I want is inside me: I decide. I am the creator. The security I was looking for is in me.

Abundance is in me. I don't have anything to prove, because I am big the way I am.

I challenge you to make the journey from your head to your heart. Live life to the full and create your own heaven on earth for yourself. Start today!

About the Author

Cindy Vranken (Belgium) alias Mega Cindy is a heart driven sales expert with a proven track record in IT, telco and software companies. She is the founder of megacindy.com and the number 1 sales trainer for entrepreneurs. She has inspired thousands of entrepreneurs to sell from the heart through her method based on the best practises of 22 years of sales. Her soft skills she has developed as a reiki master, healer and avatar wizard.

Born To Be My Own Hero
Serife Bayar

Five years ago, I lost everything. I completely broke down. This is my story. I come from an entrepreneurial family. Ever since I can remember, my parents were always working. Every day, while my friends were playing outside, I went to daycare. I was raised with the motto: 'If you want to achieve something, you have to work very hard for it'.

My parents had a Turkish restaurant. Since my fifteenth birthday, I worked as a waitress and soon learned the skills of running a business and generating sales. At first, I wasn't paid for the work I did, but I had a deal with my father that I would get a percentage of the revenue if I managed to sell the most expensive dishes. Well, that's when I found out sales was really my thing. Making money was so much fun! I sold the most expensive meals and got the best tips. In addition, I took care of the marketing and branding and our restaurant was fully booked every evening.

All I did was make people feel comfortable, take their coats, accompany them to their seats, and ask them if they had eaten Turkish food before. Because of my recommendations, they ordered the most expensive meals.

The best part was when people felt so comfortable, they ordered a bottle of wine and, as you can imagine, the most expensive kind. When I brought the bill at the end of the evening, I added two liqueurs for free. Customers were so positive. They had a great evening with free liqueur, they always left with a big smile, and I received the biggest tips.

Born to be happy?

I believe that the key to every success story in life is to make happiness your goal. Whatever I wanted in life, I had to make it happen. Happiness started with me, not with my relationships, not with my job, not with my money, and certainly not with my circumstances, but with me. I believe everyone is born to be happy and can be successful in life; it's how you respond to situations in life, your thoughts, your goals, and your frequency to attract anything you want. To make a difference and to make it all happen, you must have a purpose.

Since I was a little girl, I always wanted to become a writer. Unfortunately, it had never been possible because magazines often found my writing style not in line with their wishes. I had made the decision to take a different direction: sales in the business world. After a while, I started as a young potential in a Dutch Telecom company. From there, I made big career steps and became one of the best sales executives in this company.

Then five years ago, I lost everything I had: my marriage, my job, my health, and my faith in people. I didn't want to get out of bed anymore. Luckily, I had a beautiful two-year old daughter who needed my care, so I was determined to make something of my life. My daughter saw me as her biggest role model and I couldn't disappoint her. I had to get back on my feet again, so I made a choice. I had to do everything that made me feel happy. I knew that when I was happy, I always attracted everything I wanted.

Inner peace

During my burn out, I felt restless, I couldn't sleep, I could no longer eat, and I was feeling tired all the time. I had no more energy. I knew that the first step to regaining my former self was to regain my inner peace. I read an article in which someone mentioned that trees and plants could cure people. To learn more, I bought a book of this so-called Bach remedy and started taking the recommended drops daily. I soon discovered that plants and flowers can, in fact, change negative emotions into positive qualities. Dr. Bach's remedies restored my inner balance and emotional well-being in a friendly and gentle manner. I finally got some sleep again and felt no anxiety.

I started taking care of myself and I started practicing yoga with my best friend. The first time, I just kept on falling over because I did not understand it. After taking a couple of lessons, I learned to balance. I noticed that my legs were getting leaner, my arms were getting stronger and, most importantly, I noticed an inner strength. In those days, I spoke to my therapist for hours and she gave me the best advice ever: reiki. This has been the best gift anyone has ever given me. Reiki, a way to heal both physically and spiritually, originated in Japan. It works through the laying of hands and it is the transmission of the universal life force energy, the power of all existence. Through reiki, I could give myself and my daughter energy with my hands. It was magical, especially the first time. I was by then a 'reiki one'.

Be your own hero

When my life felt apart, I had to first rescue myself before I could take care of my daughter. In every Disney movie, there is a prince who rescues the princess and they live happily ever after. In real life, there are no princes. So, rescue yourself; be your own hero and your biggest fan. Love yourself first because that's who you'll be spending the rest of your life with. After my burn out, the only thing I could depend on were my own wings. I was always thankful in life, even when I had nothing. I counted my blessings every day and wrote them down. I was blessed for being a mummy to the most beautiful girl; I was thankful for starting a new job; thankful for having the best friends who were there for me in my worst times and made me laugh again; and thankful for being healthy.

I went looking for the secrets to happiness and I discovered that the happiest people live in the Blue Zone islands: Sardinia in Italy, Okinawa in Japan, Loma Linda in California, Nicoya in Costa Rica, and Ikaria in Greece.

People in these areas live without stress, share happiness with their family, have a sense of purpose in life, and have a healthy dose of personal awareness. I copied a lot of their habits and added some of my own. I started to do everything I always wanted when I was a little girl. I started writing, went horse riding, had long walks on the beach, and spent a lot of time with my friends and family. My house sometimes looked like a daycare, but I didn't care. My daughter and I had the time of our lives. Achieving happiness became our motto.

Good things on their way

Yoga taught me to recite mantras, so I used affirmations in my daily life that really changed my thinking and behavior. Every morning in my car, I called out these affirmations: 'Every day I grow stronger and I can get through anything.' 'I am free of worry and peace right now.' 'Something awesome is going to happen to me.' 'I believe good things are on their way.' 'I have a lot to be thankful for.' 'I make good choices.' 'Everything I want is entering my life.' Every night, I talked to the moon. I know it may sound silly, but the moon has so much energy to give. I asked for new energy in my life and it arrived. I asked for a new job and got it. I asked if I could win a writing competition and I won. I also learned the technique of visualizing. I made a vision board with all my wishes and dreams. After a while, all my dreams came true. I started with a detox for my body, but also for my life. To feel happy again, detox everything in life that is not good for you, like materialism, toxic plants, and unhealthy food. I even started detoxing my life from people who gave me bad vibes. When I discarded the things in my life that no longer served me, I felt free again.

Be the best version of yourself

I can say the past few years have been a crazy ride. During my journey, I've learned so much about life. I grew in my development, in my thinking, and in my behavior. Now I live my life as I never have before and I really get everything out of it. Whenever opportunities arise, I respond to them. During my darkest times, I never complained.

I never stopped dreaming or believing. I just continued to look for ways to feel good. When I continuously felt good, happiness flowed back into my life again. I attracted new friends, I was inspired to carry on writing, and happiness became a way of life.

In the meantime, more and more entrepreneurs came to ask if I could help them with their writing and with their sales. I discovered there was a huge demand for good public relation advice, especially from people with an ethnic background. And that's how my company 'Sales & Branding', was born. It's five years later and I am living in the house of my dreams, I have paid off all my debt, and I am back on my feet. I still work for a telecom company as partner manager, but I also have my own company. I can say with confidence and gratitude that I love my life and it is perfect.

But the best part is that my daughter is fantastic with loads of confidence and a talent for singing and dancing. She takes theatre and ballet classes and shines on the stage when she performs. She is not afraid of anything. I always tell her how proud I am of her and ask her, 'Why are you so fantastic?' She always responds with the same sentence: 'That's because I have the coolest mommy in the world.'

About the Author

Serife Bayar (Netherlands) is owner of the company 'Sales & Branding'. Her personal journey has taught her that by making happiness her life goal, she can achieve anything. She has since helped entrepreneurs discover their happiness and fulfill their purpose in business and in life.

All About Eve
Eve van Dijk

'She was nine when her mother left her. School exasperated her; she was shy and invisible. As an adult, she survived breast cancer when she was 46. With a Master's degree in tax law, she was a tax adviser and a professional coach in women's leadership. She started communities for literature lovers, musicians, and colleagues. She was a caregiver to her mother-in-law. Today, she has a company supporting caregivers and advising big organisations on implementing caregiver-friendly staff policies.'

Yet in the first twenty years of my life, I was lonely. Nobody listened to me. Nobody saw me.

I was born in 1960, the first-born to my parents. A small-town middle-class family in the Netherlands. My parents did not speak to each other, except when they quarrelled. My way of surviving was to be invisible and feel nothing. It helped that I was a shy girl who preferred reading in my own room where it was quiet.

My father was an engineer in a big steel factory. He always went out after work because of his many adventure-seeking hobbies, we did not see him often. He was a great storyteller and I loved his stories. But he did not listen to my stories, so I told myself am not worth listening to. My little brother who had minor brain injury, kept my mother so busy that she had hardly enough energy for cleaning the house or paying attention to me and my younger sister.

Books were my best friends. I was hungry for knowledge, so I became a hard-working, diligent pupil. I had a school friend, Karin, who always had me laughing out loud because she acted like a clown. One day, I laughed so much that I peed in my pants. The next day at school, Karin moved her table away from mine and stopped speaking to me. She told the other children that I had fleas, meaning that I was filthy, which wasn't true. That was the end of our friendship. As a child, I did not understand her sudden change in behaviour. I was left heartbroken.

Over the years, I developed a million sensors that I used to judge people. A raised eyebrow could make me feel uncertain; 'He likes me...he likes me not.' It made me a good observer.

What would you really like to do?

When my teacher asked what I wanted to be when I grew up, I answered: 'I want to be a teacher.' Her response changed my life completely: 'Oh, no! You can do much better than that.' So I decided not to become a teacher. Not sure what to do, I went to law school after graduating from high school. When I was twenty, my father advised me to choose tax law because 'you will have a good job with a great salary.' I followed his advice and after seven years, I had a Master's degree in law. In the seven years that followed, I worked as a tax adviser for different companies and I had a great salary. But I was not happy. Honestly, tax law was not my favourite thing. To make matters worse, I didn't like the other tax advisers. I was not 'one of the guys'. This time around, it was not them not liking me, but rather me not liking them. I felt different. I didn't care much for a bigger car or a bigger house with a swimming pool. So what, then, did I care about?

What I cared most about in life was spending time with others. I cared about people being attentive to each other, laughing and crying together, having fun together, and enjoying each other's company. I cared about friends and being there when someone needed me. I cared about telling my story to someone who listened. To be happy, I needed to leave behind my exasperated inner-child and become a woman with a voice.

My husband, Rob, was the one person who helped me through this. He encouraged me to talk to people, to show my feelings, and to openly discuss my doubts and insecurities. I could listen, so I was good company, but it was time to learn to talk. I needed to convince myself that my story mattered and that it was worth telling. I needed to believe that I was allowed to take up space. For the first time in my life, someone listened to me. Wow! After eleven years of courtship, Rob and I married, and we had a son and a daughter. I'm now the mother I never had. I love my family and they love me. We show our love by sharing our stories and listening to each other.

Two years after I gave birth to my daughter, I started to miss work. But what could I do? I was a tax law graduate who didn't like being a tax lawyer. For a while, I did whatever came along, including volunteering at a day care centre for children, interviewing for scientific research, and advising start-up entrepreneurs. In early 2006, someone asked me a life-changing question: 'Eve, what would you really like to do?' 'Listen to people', I answered.

I went to the School for Coaching and Training and started my own coaching company: A-Pro-Pos Coaching. I coached women who wanted to be in charge of their own lives. During this time, I encountered various other challenges. In April 2006, my mother had a stroke. In the ten years before, we had not spoken to each other. After the stroke, we renewed our relationship. In 2007, I was diagnosed with breast cancer. I needed two rounds of surgery before I was in the clear. Thankfully, I have now been cancer-free for over ten years. On April 5th of 2008, my father died. Exactly nine months later, on January 5th of 2009, my mother died. Although my parents and I didn't have the warmest of relationships, I mourned their passing.

In between my two surgeries, I had one coaching client who was my rock. Coaching her helped me through this tough time. One positive aspect of surviving breast cancer is that I became kinder to myself. I learnt to take life less seriously and I allowed myself to have more fun. With my newfound sense of purpose, I decided to do only the things I really enjoyed doing. I also became aware of another skill. Besides listening and observing, I realised I was a natural match-maker: I have a gift of bringing together people with challenges and those with the solutions. This skill comes so naturally to me that it took me years to realise it.

Taking care

With all these skills and my need to be seen and heard, I created various groups. With my friends, I started a book club and a group for musicians. With my coaching colleagues, I started a sparring group. Through these groups, I have surrounded myself with people who like each other and get along because I chose them. All these groups are more than eight years old and still going strong. During spring of 2014, my mother-in-law broke her hip at 91-years of age. After four weeks of being hospitalised and six weeks of recovering in a health centre, she needed a mobility walker. Her 93-year-old partner had to take care of her 24 hours a day and soon this became far too difficult for him. I remember when he first asked me: 'Eve, when you do your shopping, will you please bring us half a loaf of white bread?' And so, our period of caregiving started.

It began with a small question. Of course, we helped them because they were Rob's parents, but not long after that first small request we found ourselves doing all the shopping and cleaning their house. We didn't mind doing it, except that the longer it took, the more energy it required from Rob. He visited his mother every day because she lived on the way home from his work, which made it even more demanding. After several months, Rob was so tired he fell asleep on the couch every evening. Slowly, I lost my husband. It almost meant the end of our marriage because I felt I was in the same situation as when my mom's attention was focused only on my brother. I wasn't being seen and I wasn't being heard by my husband anymore. Once again, I felt lonely.

Despite the negativity during that period, something positive came out of it. Because I only had a few coaching clients at that time, I had time to keep my mother-in-law company when her partner wanted to go out by himself. When I was with her, he could leave the house without worrying. After she died at Christmas in 2014, I wondered if there were companies offering a service to replace the regular caretaker for a couple of hours a day. There was, but not in the area where I lived. After a little research, I started a support company for caretakers: Kappa Helpt! (Kappa Helps!). When spoken in Dutch, 'Kappa' sounds like the words cape and kapel (chapel) which mean protection and safety.

Today, we have sixteen employees who keep the old and sick company. We also sit in for the regular caregivers so that they have time to carry on with some of their regular activities - such as spending time with their partners, doing household chores, and catching up on their hobbies - knowing the ones they care about are in safe hands. It allows them more time to be present with their families; it gives them more time to listen. In addition, we advise big organisations on how to implement caregiver-friendly staff policies.

Fortunately, I have a positive mindset. Shit happens. What matters is how you deal with it: you can choose to be a victim or a hero. You can wait till someone comes to rescue you, but they may never appear. Sometimes, you need to rise above yourself. Begin somewhere. It doesn't matter where. During your life, you will discover your skills. You will develop them along the way until just the right moment when you can use them to help other people.

About the Author

Eve van Dijk (Netherlands) is the founder and owner of Kappa Helpt!, a company that supports caregivers. She is also the founder and owner of Mevrouw Van Dijk (Mrs Van Dijk), a company that advises big organisations on how to implement caregiver-friendly staff policies. Connecting people is in her nature. She is happily married to Rob, who will support her in her business when he retires. They have a son, a daughter, and two cats.

Giving Up Is Not An Option
Ayse Top

Accountant. My father wanted me to have the best possible future and that is why I had to study to become an accountant. He reasoned that it would pay well, and thereby chose the path my life would follow. I was a young, shy girl who dreamed of typical girly things like fashion and beauty, and I was up against a demanding father with high expectations about school performance. I faithfully did what was required of me because going against my father was not possible. And because the bar was so high, I faced stress, frustration and fear when I had to tell him about poor school results.

The world of accountancy was not for me; it did not feel right and it did not make me happy. I dropped out during my first year and decided to resume my studies in a year's time in the hope that I would be more motivated.

Number One

In the meantime, I had found a job as a data-entry employee, but all the numbers I had to enter daily also just swam before my eyes. I went back to school but not for the accountancy training. I successfully completed a secretarial course and many types of jobs followed. But with every new employer the feeling of disappointment also grew. I felt disappointed because it was just 'a job' and it lacked 'a goal'. I had never envisaged this future for myself.

At 29 years old, I took stock of my life up to that moment. I had to conclude that, because of my upbringing, I had certainly never stood up for myself. I always let the interests of others come first and I had not achieved anything myself. I felt pretty bad. But what a great discovery! Now that I saw it so clearly, I decided to change my direction drastically. Giving up was not an option. I would get rid of all the negative feelings about myself. From now on I would deal with things differently. From now on I would be number one.

Go for it!

And all those early dreams about fashion and beauty would become reality. That was my future. I wanted to operate independently, start my own company. And because I had also become a mother, I wanted to combine my new activities with my children's school schedule.

An opportunity immediately materialized through a friend. She drew my attention to the application of eyelash extensions, which around 2010 in the Netherlands was a yet-unknown phenomenon. With the artificial eyelashes, I was a trendsetter and acquaintances and total strangers complimented me. In the mirror I saw a magical glance and in many ways my eyes were opened. I knew exactly what I wanted: to make women more confident with beauty products.

I took a course to become an eyelash stylist and the assignments poured in. Apparently, I had hit a soft spot in women. The feeling of working with a goal was fantastic; I was on the right track. I made plans, worked them out and showed them to my family and acquaintances. I wanted those around me to see that what I had always dreamed about had turned out to be true. Unfortunately, I also got a lot of opposition from those around me. Apparently not everyone felt the same way about it. But that did not bother me. I persevered even when problems came along. Nothing could get me down; I was unstoppable now. 'Beauty Department' became the name of my very own company.

Things were not going well at the call center where I was working at that moment, so I left. The financial consequences of this did not bother me because what had started out as a side job to earn extra income had quickly grown to the point that I was opening my own business location in Utrecht, one of the largest cities in the Netherlands. My business at that first location specialized in eyelash extensions and other beauty products. And because I could now really go for it, I also invested more time in my business. As a result, the customer base grew tremendously. I was earning my own money doing what I liked the most! And this was also when my youngest child started going to elementary school.

Success and failure

Soon I needed reinforcement and so I took on an employee. When it appeared that the first location had become too small, I moved to a larger business location. The number of customers, however, enormously fell when I moved again without properly assessing the location of the property. The poor location and accessibility cost me customers. I spent quite a lot of money on marketing and advertising but that could not turn the tide. I was forced to choose a more central location. This also involved many necessary costs. I learned an important lesson in basic entrepreneurship by naively focusing on a beautiful exterior.

Those first years of entrepreneurship had even more important lessons in store for me. Because things had gone so well, I had developed an urge to grow even more. I really wanted to take over an existing business in Amsterdam. Therefore, I was often away from my business and I let people I trusted run the business for me. That turned out to be a mistake. Decisions were made without my involvement and I should have paid more attention to the accounting. To make a long story short, the business in Utrecht went bankrupt and the takeover in Amsterdam was canceled because the other party did not fulfill its promise. It was terrible and I had to start all over again, because giving up was not an option. I did, however, learn my lesson from this. I would have to exercise a lot more control and make strict business agreements with everyone.

'Look before you leap' is one of the most important lessons that I have learned here. And after all the setbacks, the people who hurt me and the many trials and errors, I now have four beautiful businesses with locations in the Netherlands and one in Belgium. Each one has the right team of employees to continue moving forward. I am proud of myself. I am the owner and I train others.

'Ladies and gentlemen... Mrs. Netherlands Universe 2018!'

And when everything is running smoothly, you receive even more. In 2017, I was asked to participate in the Mrs. Netherlands Universe 2018 competition. I was thrilled when I won the competition. The preparatory period brought me a wealth of personal growth, knowledge and insights. I am grateful for the opportunity I was given and grateful that I was able to fully develop myself. And of course, my beauty centers continued to do well. In December 2018 I will participate in the Mrs. Universe 2018 competition in the Philippines. The experience will certainly enrich my life.

The Mrs. Netherlands Universe competition has a good cause: 'Stop Domestic Violence Against Women'. Of course, I am an ambassador for this. In addition, I also contribute in my own way to making women financially independent. On the first day of each month, a woman can win a free course at Beauty Department. The course increases the independence and self-awareness of the women. These are exactly the two elements that I also eagerly wished for when my father chose the role of accountant for me. By the way, my father's parenting style is very different from my own. I will advise my children and support their choices.

I have followed my heart and chosen my own vocation and I have not let anyone stop me. I am a happy woman and I know what I want. I did it my way.

About the Author

Ayse Top (Netherlands) is owner of a range of companies in the beauty sector, from eyelash treatments to weight loss, in the Netherlands and Belgium. She is mother of three children and Mrs. Netherlands Universe 2018.

Printed in Great Britain
by Amazon